Future, Former, Fugitive

Future, Former, Fugitive

by Olivier Cadiot

translated by Cole Swensen

Roof Books
New York

ISBN: 0-931824-09-6
Library of Congress Catalog Card No.: 2003096461

Acknowledgments
Published originally in French as *Futur, ancien, fugitif* by P.O.L, Paris,
France.

Sections have previously appeared in *Psalm* and
The Yale Anthology of Twentieth Century French Poetry

The translator would like to thank the author as well as Babette Miles,
Jennifer Pap, and Jean-Jacques Poucel for their generous help.

Roof Books are distributed by
Small Press Distribution
1341 Seventh Avenue
Berkeley, CA 94710-1403
Phone orders: 800-869-7553
www.spdbooks.org

State of the Arts This book was made possible, in part, with public funds from
the New York State Council on the Arts, a state agency.
NYSCA

ROOF BOOKS
are published by
Segue Foundation
303 East 8th Street
New York, NY 10009
www.roofbooks.com

CONTENTS

The Shipwreck

Mr. and Mrs. ***
request the pleasure of the company of

_____
for dinner
on _____

Mm, and how are you my dear Mrs. Ramplee-Smith?
I am ever so happy oh to see you
But? Yes! what?

[inaudible]

Oh very good perfect oh splendid!
And I do hope that your family is doing well
if not I'm so sorry to hear it yes of course naturally
What?
[little cries, gasps, grindings of teeth]

But here everything's changed it's not at all like before
oh but the furniture's all new and these colors
Simply marvelous
And this arrangement this ensemble it's so
No really it's fantastic what style what (...)
How do you do it?

How's everything Mrs. Jones?
How's everything Mrs. Jones?
Or: Hello Mrs. Jones, lovely day, isn't it?
I really couldn't say

[blunder #1]
oh excuse me

Frankly no one no
no one told me no one
no one told me anything of the sort
what a shame!

[aside]
You'll pay for this one
You'll pay for this one
this scene = bad-bad
Back up
go around the back way
spiral through the branches
slant across the path

hedge path hedge path hedge

So-r-r-r-y yes really or:
I beg your pardon
I-beg-yo-ur-par-don
Believe me sincerely truly, your etc.

Oh I want it all to be like this forever
Oh I want it all to be like this forever

Ah my dear
Dear Sir,
It is with pleasure that
So receive accept believe dear Sir,
in my deepest respects [sinking into the sofa
<oooof>]
Your so devoted loyal entirely yours
your friend—

SPINACH SOUFFLE AND BRAINS
EEL WITH LEEKS
GUINEA FOUL IN ASPIC
BLACK CHERRIES

This dog! he's driving me nuts prowling around me
around and around like that
tell him to stay cccccalm good lord
this dog oh this dog
Please stop stop STOP

Ok I'll stay
conclusion yes
your yes dear Mrs. *** your (yours by His Grace)
your thoroughly and completely

loyal friend and servant
and I have [raising his glass] the honor to: etc.
I'm gonna kill him one of these days I'm gonna kill him
[aside]
Shush! to make the final toast in your—uh to dedicate
this and that and all I've done so there [drinking].

Mr. *** [standing to speak]: *** has been built on the foundations of an ancient Roman reservoir—you can still see the excavations deep in the forest .... and so the water, welling up from natural springs, still feeds the system of canals—and an extremely ingenious one at that—which distributes water throughout the ornamental sections and turns a wheel on the other side that in earlier times operated numerous useful machines for the garden...
..... and what was once the dungeon has now been transformed into small apartments—oh they were filthy beyond belief if you had only seen them—instantly recalling their original purpose— look at these frescos they found beneath the paint here and it was filthy perfectly filthy—

Me.
The excavations are surrounded by poplars
this way
excuse me

hedges
branches
brambles

this way

in my day
ducks fish birds tadpoles
squirrels deer crayfish hornets

A real virgin forest, no?
this way
after you
                    [skipping along]

strawberries
roses
acacias

Bzzz the cows Bzzz the cows Bzzz
the flies Bzzz
Bzzz

I don't speak
I don't say a word
I hold my tongue
                              [aside]
the flies
Bzzz

Latrines behind the wall
green planks moss hole
and it disappeared

                              into the water
after
Oh excuse me
[blunder #2]
I didn't say that I swear it
I pray you'll find it in your heart to forgive me
good God for my extreme stupidity
[more and more anguish in the voice]
for it was unpardonable I fear Truly
I fear utterly and completely

In short:
I confess that I was terribly nervous
without a doubt, yes—nervous, yes
or simply:
1. I am sad because of what I've done
2. I am solely and utterly to blame
It was I; it was my fault
Very sincerely yours
so there.

Good
oh look at the time! Oh dear! goodbye thank you
see you all soon goodbye Bob (or Mary)
the dog to all a good night
again forgive me for what I have done
to all again please forgive everything in sight
I-I wanted
who would have believed (consider: Why I always make mistakes)

I would like
simply to thank you as much as I would have liked God willing
Thank you, believe me, etc.

It's already night no more noise the day dissolved nothing left
barking distant voices dissipated nothing
nothing left so long

goodbye
nothing
darkness

goodbye
nothing
darkness.

2.   WHY I ALWAYS MAKE MISTAKES

I had accepted the invitation in spite of my reservations. Why go back into the past and risk igniting old memories—bitter vivid sad intact—why? And yet I went back there as you know from the above, before making certain decisions whose tragic consequences you'll see below. To go back in order to learn more about certain situations and to make some decisions in full knowledge of the causes. Healthy of mind, sure of purpose, determined as in everything.

So I had to return because I had forgotten it all owing to "the enormous space of time." Granny always said you don't remember much and she was certainly right. How utterly classic and rather banal to want to understand things today in light of the past.

This place had to be—it's what was predicted and what everyone believed— the site of an edifying life, and it's there so to speak that I had to find the wherewithal to recreate myself as they say *my beloved has gone down into the garden* or *life is nothing but a storm of thorns* (remember: The Sermons of Felix). To recreate myself = to have an identity—which is to say, "a character"—of which I will be proud in the future. A complete education, which he is far from possessing at the moment (background laughter) isn't that so my boy? .... Continuation of the sermon: *Because we refuse him bread when he comes clothed in the body of the poor who are his limbs and whoever loves his peace must flee such a storm of* etc. etc.

[slight coughs, throats clearing, chairs creaking]
I understood absolutely nothing. I don't know what they mean by a "complete education," I only know that I have been mistreated *laudate pueri dominum* and you have to be like a child to understand *you try to make a character for yourself you poor fool you try for originality no one's going to believe you* **OK fine and then?** [shouted]

They also said that you're here to recover your health—false, utterly false! noted: 1. the lack of exercise 2. the imposed diet (and I can prove it). No field, no space set aside for that. Nothing: already still life no birds no plants no sky (remember: Natal-grey).

In this particular case (pointing at me) in this "difficult" case—which is to say a battle in a pure state—what is gained by one is lost by the other. The loss exactly matches the gain. Result theoretically nil, but fruitful in terms of training [incredulous stares from the family].

Most important, I understood nothing—and I defy any reasonable person to explain it—of the phrases—and that's just one example, let's not even get into the others—such as *the spouse of a word has an animal's body* or *the spouse of eternal life still lives among the dead* or even *the divine song of birds (piiiii-iiii) is essentially arbitrary.*

True, I then had to rid myself of all this muddle of accumulated words. It was no longer enough to cry out absurd things like Glaaaaz-ziiier to make them disappear. And like Granny said, remember it's the horse that jumps not you, which roughly translates as: he who has nothing has nothing, he who risks nothing has nothing, and he who does nothing does nothing, so I decided to go.

Leaving was not a betrayal—or rather let's say it only ended up that way. It's only later that one sees these things, Granny said and she was right. Only much later did I realize that certain things were expected of me that I didn't do. But I did other things *you did nothing it's all lies you haven't moved you haven't changed you haven't done a thing* (...) and that required a certain courage *liar that's wrong liar* to uh to do all that and to maintain a decent daily life *liar* **I have done what I have done, I have done what I could** [shouted].

I had accepted this invitation in order to observe the place and come to some conclusions. They were negative. I set out *false false that's entirely false you haven't done a thing you haven't budged* **the crossing was excellent** *you're prevaricating* **the crossing was excellent** until the moment when there I was suddenly all alone on this island *no but this is the journal of a madman!* **hold your tongue** relieved of all these words and memories (add here: Why I hear voices) from which I justifiably sought to liberate myself by leaving.

3.   MY LIFE IN ***.

Felix (the tutor):

1. Grave voice and circles under the eyes.
2. Slight trembling of the hands and lips (drooling a little from the corner).
3. Brusque tonic accent on unimportant words to dissipate fear. Seems to stutter.
4. Launches into interminable digressions.
5. Is successful when singing.
6. Focuses on sententious phrases to learn them by heart.
7. Calls me dry fruit unfit zero.

I'm only telling this for your own good yes yes it's exactly the same with your brother yes yes though with him I had less to repair .... he's a charlatan [me]. Besides you shouldn't be so lax with him. He's a rotten branch, an error of nature, a deviation—they knew this was a bit of an exaggeration but they let it pass, seduced as they were by his methods.

We didn't know if he was young or old; he was a well-preserved specimen. You can forget about time but it won't forget about you Granny said, and for once she was wrong, for it—time—had completely forgotten him. And that gave me the impression that I too was an embryo ad vitam.

You couldn't say that the *re-education* sessions with him were any vacation.

EXAMPLE

Me. If, for example, in the evening I'm told to go somewhere and do something, I'll forget it all by the next day, but I don't do it on purpose, that's for sure.
Him. I'm happy to hear that you don't do it on purpose, but it's no excuse.
Me. In fact, the next day, if I have time, you know, well, then I'll do it—I don't forget completely.
Him. Ah, so you *do* do it on purpose, which proves that you simply don't *want* to do it. And who asks you to do these things anyway?
Me. "They" ask me.

19

Him. And who are "they?"

Me. Forgotten it's forgotten and not like it could come back it's gone.

Him. Listen to me kid, I'm going to tell you something. What is gained on the one hand is lost on the other. The rat eats spiders who eat fleas who eat the cat...

Me. Ha ha ha.

Him. Oh so that makes you laugh, does it? OH SO THAT MAKES YOU LAUGH. You poor little creep. Oh no no mercy for you! hopeless!!! [he trembles with fury] no no no ... ... they'll bring you back down to earth. Locked up shut away done for. You'll start by going to see Mr. ***, that'll teach you.

Me. I-I b-but...n-no

Him. That's just the beginning and believe me it'll be good. Made to order. By hand. Especially.

4.   ROBINSON'S FIRST WORDS.

Day One.

grewn griel grace grob gran grette gri gro green grad grouet gra gre grel grill gruel gra groin gron greek gremme graft groil grai grip grage grave gryeu grien graze grin groun grew

Day Two.

Go no so rapanpam lajafadaba pi vi mi dizirilibiti
You too fou rufubu vusupumujudu
Vo ro jo botopolodo
Delepetebe femere venerejese

Day Three.

Mosquito morning marriage
Boi-li-ng bea-stl-y po-k-ing
Sw-ea-r-ing em-er-ald em-arv-el

Cru-nc-hing coc-kle cro-w
Critical cre-ature
Un-vei-ling mor-e of m-ust

Gra-zi-ng en-gor-gin-g g-rav-i-ty

Day Four.

1. Inability to walk or stand upright.
2. Loss of voice.
3. Local paralysis and waking dreams.
4. Amnesiac gaps.
5. Lucid muteness.
6. Twilight states.
7. Answers not related to questions.
8. Wrong answers to simple questions: how many fingers do I have? *Six.*
9. Move naked / move forward / naked / move naked / move forward / arms naked / naked / and so on.
10. Repeated washings + hiding things to search for them later *but where* groaning *could I have possibly put it?*
11. Precisely repeating a given operation before any action.
12. Fixed idea sine materia. *I want nothing/I want everything.*
13. Delirious illusions of being loved.
14. Notion of royal connections.
15. Influence *whoever is across from me is beaming me things.*
16. The faculty of thought taken over *it's not I who thinks, they are making me think.*
17. Commentary accompanying action *look, he's standing up, look, he's going to leave etc.* without stopping and accompanied by insults (see: The B.T.W. syndrome–bitch-tart-whore).
18. The Delirious Inventor.
19. The forced act.

Day Six

1. The delirium of negation *nothing exists anymore and everything exists eternally in me.*
2. Unheard of crimes.
3. Discordant ideas.
4. Telegraphic style.
5. Astonishment of the organism *something inside me is burning.*
6. Ordering food without the means to pay for it.
7. Professional dreams.
8. Stiff neck.
9. Thirst for action.
10. The danger of sudden death.
11. Collapse of the will *I'm not what I was before.*
12. The body leaning forward.
13. Notions of ruin and incurability.

14. The raptus of ***.
15. Marble features.
16. Threat of a relapse.
17. Stylization of natural acts and doubling of the voice.

5.   MY LIFE IN *** (CONTINUED).

Each morning I did the required exercises. Often a course in theory preceded the practical work.

EXAMPLE

– AAAh [he held out his hand then quickly closed it, pointing his thumb toward his mouth]. What does that mean?
– (...)
– That means I'm thirsty. File it away in your brain—there's no magic to it. Which therefore implies that:
1. Inarticulate language is not so natural. Which also contradicts your blind faith—if I may phrase it thus—in your primitiveness. And no you were not found in a forest!
2. But to have learned is nothing more than to know something at some point that you hadn't known at a prior point.
3. We're reduced to judging the meaning of words by the circumstances in which we hear them. Often we never get beyond an approximate understanding.
– (...)? [he groans an order in my direction]
– (...) [I imitate his earlier gesture]
– Ok so you're thirsty my friend!
– (...)
– Ok so drink! [he takes a flask from his pocket]
– ...[I drink and then spit out the contents]
– Hahaha [he howls with laughter].

6.   LETTERS & TRANSLATED FROM MY NATIVE LANGUAGE

Mr. and Mrs. Christopher King
regret exceedingly regret terribly
that a sudden and severe illness
that a sudden and terrible that an unexpected and veritable
illness in their family

illness in <u>their</u> family here right where we are
but entirely free of their will
obliges implies the infinite displacement
the expectation of something
1. whose outcome is certain
2. and whose duration is not fixed
fixed foreseen prearranged
(like the arrangement of tables the flowers the service)
the 12th inst. the 12th of the present month
again please forgive us oh please
oh will you really and believe etc.

My dear Mrs. ***,
An accident in the water yesterday
(an accident in the water?)
resulted in such a severe sprain
that I fear I am terribly afraid that it will be impossible to be present
impossible to appear—Oh—at your table tomorrow
the excruciating pain in the injured ankle is nothing
No, no! I assure you really it's really nothing
it's nothing compared to the pain of ... uh?
No! Wait, it's:
<u>this pain is less intolerable</u>
(transitory and non-definitive)
than what I feel in abandoning in renouncing
the occasion the lost opportunity—the total
and definitive privation—of the utter joy of tasting
your always oh
So delicious hospitality
with my regrets, etc.

Dear Jack,
Why don't you come to our place for tea
on the lawn (pré) Friday the 15th? The strawberries
(les fraises et les roses) and the roses
will soon be ripe
the strawberries and the roses are ready
in their prime right now
do come
and I suggest you come prepared to adore said strawberries and roses
so similar
to those so beautiful specimens that you possess
cultivate contemplate raise with love

and are produced in your formal symmetrical historical
and entirely more marvelous than mine garden
(compliment!)
Therefore
I have informally invited on this occasion
a few true friends
meticulously selected from the rabble
whose amity though ephemeral is not altogether accidental
and if there's no adverse argument from your perspective
no! it's not that, it's:
if you have anyone staying with you at the moment
I would be oh so delighted to see her/he/him
your very dear affectionate so close your beloved
beloved be-lov-ed relative
without calling first on the spur of the moment come,
any time is perfect
Margaret V.

Dear, I was profoundly wounded injured affected
and how false these words sound
because of their feeble inability to convey the true enormity
of my sincere and overwhelming grief at this news
at this communication
at this announcement
Yes at the announcement today of the passing
of your mother and oh how well I know
dipli dipli dipli hi
oui wou no ha shairin yourloss
and little and nothing will suffice will be sufficient to say
or to write in order to assure you of the inalienable
1. eternal participation of souls
2. interaction of same
3. affectionate increase of the above sentiments
and so little not being enough to bring you
dipli dipli dipli
just a smidgen of true consolation I just cannot stop myself therefore
from assuring you of my most tender and grief-ridden
sympathy.

Ze simpati
ze simpati.

– Come out, I repeated
[I struck my palm with the bamboo switch]
Get – thwack – out – thwack – of there – thwack – thwack

– So are you coming out or not!

                                        or must I come in and get you?
– (...)
[she's perched up in the hazelnut]

                        — Among the flowers
                                who – there
                that—
                        hmm?

– What?

– It's a poeticism, it's like that.

[silence I wait a long time then]
– Good!
                        [beneath the tree]

– My God! Come out! I can see you perfectly!
– (...)
– Want to play Walter?
– Ok
[she comes down out of the tree]

– Could I speak to Sir Walter please.
– I've got to leave you'll still be here in a while?
– You're <u>mean</u> but it's time to go anyway
– Perfect day in the sky by the lake.
– NO! Da-a-y, like no wa-a-ay good lord! how many times do I have to tell you!
– (...)
– Ok, back to the beginning!

– Could I speak to Sir Walter?
– (...)
– You're mean but it's time to go!
– NO! You forgot that first I have to say *I've got to leave you'll still be here in a while?*

– Oh yeah!
– Ok ok don't start again just learn it by heart. Apply just a little bit of mem-
ory ok, after all it's you who wanted to play REMEMBER IT WAS YOU.

– oh sorry   [pretending to cry]
– All right poor thing go
                              [wringing her hands mute supplications]
– Again tomorrow oh tomorrow again
– Get out of my sight.
– Tomorrow?
– Goodbye calf cow etc.
– No!
– Goodbye, that's all goodbye.

Already the familiar black of night
black of night with nothing
night

not a breath
Nothing.

8.   THE RECEPTION.

Madame is served.

1. Do not touch the silverware unnecessarily.
2. Leave at least one hand placed on your knee.
3. Do not rock back and forth.
4. Do not eat everything on your plate.
5. Never take seconds, even if they are offered.
6. Do not bring up any subject that could cause disagreement.
7. Do not peel pears without a fork.
8. Never use a spoon for dessert (even if you've been given one).
9. Do not eat too much bread.
10. Never hold a bone in your hand.
11. Avoid commenting on the food.

Me:
– Hunting oh yes I love I love hunting etc..................... really it's great
the woods the the ....I love it's it's exhilarating, it's sublime! [blun-
der # 3]

oh the woods
[proclaiming]
oh I love the woods
somber green night transparent sounds
I love the woods
swift leafy black deep airy

Madame ***:
– Only God is sublime, and that's <u>by definition</u>. He is ridiculous [in a low
voice to her neighbor BUT I OVERHEARD] He is ridiculous [to the entire gath-
ering]
→ hysterical laughter sighs

What (...)
Poor uh (...)
Oh no but!
they're all like that you know <u>and God knows I've see them</u>
[eyes heavenward etc.]

(...) ri-di-cu-lous NO?   [re-laughter
muffled] this way please

THE SALON.

Monsieur ***:
– That which is ridiculous deserves to be laughed at. The laughable has its
good and bad points. The ridiculous has only the bad. There are those things
that have to make you laugh in order to fulfill their destiny their object their
proper end, and they are laughable and not ridiculous

Ah ah ah [everybody]

→ spitting groaning .... an object is
ridiculous because of the striking contrast between the way it is and the way
it should be
→ screams of joy and savage laughter eh, [he continued] therefore
it was <u>my great-great-grandfather</u> who distinguished the various heraldic
figures correctly listed as:
1. Natural figures: humans, animals, plants, stars, etc.
2. Artificial figures: weapons, hunting and fishing equipment,
musical instruments, tools, etc.

27

3. Figures without names: eagles with two heads, unicorns, wolf-men, etc. Example of the latter on two panels: To-day a king to-morrow nothing.

this way ....

<u>THE GARDEN</u>

clematis ivy sun wisteria fountain grass wall sun ivy fountain clematis

Me:
– Ah th th these be-be-begonias oh they're magnificent.
[blunder #4]
– Uh, yeah sure [continues Mr. ***] ideally I would have liked to have placed the squares like this [sketching a square in the air]: .... A vegetable patch a botanical garden an open courtyard and in the center a small enclosed rose garden NOT LOOKING AT ME NOT LOOKING AT ME as the fourth square.

Right? Me: [very fast] but it's already night already night look you can't see a thing anymore "between the dog and the wolf" as they say (bothered) uh well yeah soon (moving off) goodbye (waving his arms idiotically) wrong way down the alley already night dark boxwood boxwood (fast) go back again there it's there there it is.

9.   SEEN.

Psst-psst
(morning)

In little pieces the blue morning
ends of sky <u>suddenly</u> blue
suddenly the sky entirely blue <u>broad daylight</u>

piiiiii-iiii
[wake up]

Black piece by tiny piece <u>I am there</u> in the alley ooo ooo
black blacker and blacker the circular vault
<u>I am there etc.</u> (DIAGRAM: Me: X; the night: Y; the hedge: Z.)

ff-fff-fff
[evening]

Birds in a spiral the edge of the plains of
the birds amassed at the edge of spiral streams etc.
cacophanous piiii liri-liii
(response of all on the edge of)

takatss-takatss
[night]

> The sound tak the sound tak the exotic sound frogs or
> woodpecker or cicadas or termites the sound
> the exotic sound and suddenly nothing. Suddenly: nothing. Silence.

10.   WALK 428.

– uh, yeah, that's it.
– What's it? What?
– *The sound of incessant leaves* [in a low voice]
– Hey! what's that you said?
– Nothing.

[3 more steps]

– Did you know that the countryside you're looking at was once under the
sea!
– (...)
The fossils in this piece of stone prove it. NO not there! up there...look that's
it. 2 million B.C.E. And there it is, the sea! Yep, in this little bit of shell! *The
sound of incessant leaves*—What? What's that you said (...) what nothing?
But I heard you say something *the sound of incessant leaves.*

– HUH? Louder. What?
– Nothing *I'm going to kill you I'm going to kill you* [very low].
– CAN YOU HEAR THE SEA? Come on! We can hear it! can't we?
– *theincessantsoundofleaves*
– WHAT DID YOU SAY?
– Nothing.

Night already

smooth
night entirely black huge without moon black absolutely black.

Black. Me him + me. Me over there + him there + here me – under the shad-
ow – you've read the whole book? No. The black version? No. The book of
the complete secret of –
Black.

11.   HOW I LEFT.

Mmmmmagnificent. Yes everyone found it magnificent. However, nature
was only waiting for that to take it all back. Nature or antiquity because it's
enough to imagine the place invaded by thorns to recapture a sense of its
beginnings. Granny said: the house goes down and it'll go down, rest
assured. And I didn't regret a thing (consider: Why I left) the blue of the sky
looked like the blue of the sky.

Write
your name
on this paper

Write
your name
for me
on this pa-
per

It made my head spin and I really do think I fainted ....
I came to as we were heading off down the Lawrence and the crossing was
well underway (except that the material conditions were hard: work in the
hold, tremendous heat, lack of food). She, Mrs. Jones – who'd left with me
– had all the advantages of the passenger class and passed her time on the
promenade deck *oh the dog the little oh the little dog whose little dog is it?*
Oooh it's a dog yes really
oh yes it's my dog mine
it's my dog mine this dog
it's my dog.

STOP! LIE DOWN! [I bark]
– What's going on 227?
– Nothin suh [I realized I'd been talking to myself].

30

– Ok then, light the coal and shut up! [his body gleamed like a roasted pig]
Next time it'll be you that fries.
– Ok suh.

Better not to say anything – at least for a bit – that's the price you pay for
the trip. Granny always said you get nothing for nothing and she was right.

Mrs. Jones would slip me some food she'd stolen from the table. I'd make
like I was swabbing the deck and she'd discretely hand me a small sack.

– What d'ya have in that sack?
– Nothing suh.
– Show me!
– It's really nothing suh.
[he grabbed my hand and twisted until I dropped the sack]
– Pick up that sack!
[I picked it up and gave it to him]
– Who gave you this?
– No one, suh, I found it.
[I really do think I fainted]

Take a look at that, old boy
                              [the cabin pitched violently]
wind black sea black clouds
See how you can make a good boat from the trunk of a tree
                                        [showing me the book]
wind black sea
Fabulous!
                    [reproductions with scale drawings]
wind sea
                              Land [cried the lookout]
finally! Eh....fabulous!
Could you lend me this book?   **Crack**
(at that very moment)

                    Craaaaack

The affair of the sack did not attain its potential proportions because in the
following hours the boat sank and everyone who could have punished me
drowned.

Felix:
– Say anything you want, and I'll arrange it [I had no doubt that my every word was being taken down].
– Which is to say...[I lowered my head]
– So what's going on?
– I tell myself this doesn't work anymore I un-rea-son [sung in a high voice]
– I'm going to have to find a solution (...)

crack-crack [he went like this]
crack [with his hands]

– And so when I woke up I had the impression I'd been through a real ordeal.
– A real ordeal?
– Yeah.
– No doubt it's an inside/outside affair [he drew diagrams on the blackboard that I didn't understand].
– Go f— yourself Sir, I said.

That's how it was every morning *wake up Robinson*
me [weakly] it's raining it's windy and
what? run? No.
A morning like every other morning
dull grey. Run? No.
never rather stay stay
wake up Robinson
go away no go away I'm staying here.

Nothing I'm staying here no I'm sleeping no nothing go away no leave me DON'T TOUCH MY THINGS sky blue night windows go away I'm sleeping curled up in bed buried white.

Don't move don't leave escape into head hot sheet no nothing and it's like that DON'T TOUCH MY THINGS *oh oh Sir Robinson* the voice so small no. And you'll see everything you've thought since the beginning change in light of the new findings. It'll be good.

Nothing I'm staying no I'm sleeping go away no sky blue night windows DON'T TOUCH MY THINGS don't leave escape into head. And so you'll see the very things you want to forget precisely return.

Plac plac plac
– Huh?
[she's back up in the hazelnut tree]

> – *So high*
> *among the flowers*
> *blue*
>
> *funera. absol.*
> *blue*

– What is it?
– It's a poetry.
– Ah!
– <u>It's like that.</u>
– All right then I refuse, she cried tearing out the ferns
No! no! I don't want
air!

– (...)
– What? WHAT?
– Nothing.

– Psst!
– What!
– Want to play Walter again?
– Go play Walter again we're playing Walter.
– Ok, here we go.
– Who are you? [I shook her hand] Are you the one who discovered the
body?
– Yes.
[pretend to examine: blood stains etc.]

– I n-never did that! I s-s-swear it! Never. I-I d-didn't.
– I'll forget everything you say and you forget the name S.
– Ok.
– As soon as I have anything important to tell you, I'll let you know.
– Very good.
– See you soon.
– Great, see you soon.

– By the way, what's your name?
– S.
– NO! that's exactly what you must not say.
– I'm sorry [she pretends to cry] don't don't
– I think it would be better to stop.
– No, please.
– Goodbye.
– No.
– Tsk-tsk, it's over. Goodbye my lovely!

[after having added several "Tsk-tsk's" and a few "what a scene!"s, I went back to the house]

Tsk-tsk
It was dark outside.

14.   **VERY OLD MEMORY 1.**

Oh the baby to his mother
Oh the baby how sweet he is oh the baby
now that's a baby now that's a baby now that's a baby

and who is this baby
and who is **this baby** and who is this baby
and it's who

and it's a baby here
and it's this **baby here** yes
oh yes
it-'s-the-ba-by
it's my baby
it's my baby

[ad lib.]

Blue pot
white napkin
grey wall
Pale deep marine?

Blue pot
Flowers dragons
on the white napkin
emblazoned embroidered united?

Grey walls
light lacquered mouse
grey
natural painted fresco?

WATCH OUT THERE HE IS

[he is so tall he's going to break the skylight]

Come in! yes yes come in...Wou-uld-you-uh-li-ke?
an egg or something?
                                        Sure
have you **yeah yeah** shut up! have you seen X?
no
not at all

Oh no I haven't seen X. No
                                Oh good **yeah yeah** shut up oh very good great
Thanks and very good oh stop but he's going to break the the (...)
oh la la **Watch out** oh there you are it's broken there it is but no it's no big
deal no
Sorry goodbye pardon me.

1. I was invited to this place.
2. There XYZ happened.
3. I've come to investigate before disappearing.
4. I'm consulting original documents.

5. I'm disappearing.

It wasn't so much the physical work that made me suffer at the time but the low morale. As if the corporeal eyes illuminated without while they blinded within *made like a hedge around your ears* in the same way that *any of our actions that don't represent death and the new life are illegitimate actions.* Granny used to say that our words are certainly not without silence and vice-versa, and she was right. A red and green flag is neither red nor green. *I don't love him I hate him equals it's not he that I love* STOP *it's she who loves him* STOP *I hate him because he hates me* STOP STOP

silence

It was in those little songs about nothing at all that I found the solution. It's true that a series of constraints left no more room <u>one</u> for boring memories and <u>two</u> for lines spoken at that moment.

– What's your song say? [Felix asked me]
– Oh all sorts of things. Each person finds...oh well
– No, but what's it saying exactly? [he draws arrows on the blackboard]
– It's not that. It's more...the other way.
– But you don't understand anything, you're incapable, etc.

It's true that I was neither brilliant nor healthy. In any case I was complete-ly exhausted. The proof: I mumbled idiocies under my breath all day long.

Perfect day
    in the sky color close to the lake
jonquils

– blues
in the background unfurled infinity

light boat
ray-finned fish moving in the direction of the slanting bottom
the direction of their slant

– or simply
he was carried away?

So high place
– the flowers
funere.
            – absol.

there
below
there

in the meadow
– cold sweat
the stag the hare the deer

swimming between
living
underwater grasses
horse-movement
inebriation

clouds upside-down
among the flowers

– who tenderness

who
up to the waist

Follow
the bottom of the river
"advice of a friend"

Oh the (...) hasn't he
(...) disappeared

baby girl
in the grass
– disappeared

Go away you know nothing about it
go
eat leaves!
poor***

The Island

It's birdsong that wakes me violently "brings me to my feet" (reflect: Why I always have nightmares) the flock of birds sweeps upward in a high spiral at the edge of the cliffs the sound reverberates against the natural wall they form (remember: The birds of Asia enclosed in the courtyard as if in an aviary) the sound in a spiral turning as if over a lake as if in a courtyard as if in a sphere.

Fff-fff-ffff-fff the sounds grow among the angles of the courtyard (remember: First polyphonies) or sound together if they come together – the birds – in the huge dense central tree under which you could sit and whose fine close leaves like those of an ash or an acacia (see: Trees, their essence) leave the rest of the courtyard white luminous empty.

So it's birdsong that wakes me – just like before – to put it simply, for there are also other reasons for awakening – and one begins immediately to decide yes to decide and to speak and that's that.

No it's not time don't move   Low voice

Come on it's time let's get going   .

No   Agitation
Come on let's get going and cut the flack.

We'll take <u>eyes</u> a small and easy exercise. The theme of the day: EYES.

(...)

EYES, it's easy. It's something familiar.

Tie a bandana over your eyes pull   Hoarse voice
something back straining
a bowstring a bow a cross bow
a spring the wind the wind the the sails

That's excellent. On the right track. It's not so hard *it's not time nothing's started I'm sleeping I haven't woken up You're wrong* STOP! *I'm sleeping I haven't woken up I'm sleeping I haven't woken up* STOP!

And I stretch out and I sleep my back turned to the wall breathing air fff-
ffffff and some of the things I've said *you're talking to yourself you're talk-
ing to yourself* come back to me like pulling something back with effort a a
spring the wind and I've got to shout other things to fall asleep me all alone
on this island me all alone on this island the organized dream the organized
life *sleep all's well sleep* like Wings wings of certain birds me all alone on
this island Hallelujah snap birds movement Hallelujah snap movement and
I sleep so deeply.

2.   DREAM 1.

Oh she cried B. is more beautiful than I! I will avenge myself and from that
day on she detested her daughter.

The poisoned gift!
B no longer loved A who loved C who in turn hated A.

A falling leaf threw her into utter fear *she set off at a run* the sharp stones
shredding her feet she ran up against what she thought was a root and it was
the steps of a house.

Who's been sitting in my chair?
Who's been eating from my plate?
Who's been drinking from my glass?
Who's been sleeping in my bed?

Not me it was somebody else!
Story of one who left to learn fear. The young man looks all around and sees
nothing *get me out of here get me out of here* cried the voice.

After all said he much later he said maybe true
X is in danger
we've got to get him out of there
let's get going (he's already been changed into a...)

Too late
turned to stone
locked in

it was he and at the same time not he.

So there you have it oh *she is more beautiful than I* good. Is there someone more beautiful than I? Oh yes, it's B. All right okay big deal *so she's more beautiful than I* okay (implied: just wait).

there is no coat for B.
there are no gloves for B.
there is nothing left for B.

What's to be done?
OH WELL WE'LL WORK IT OUT that's all
but what difference does it make?
STOP stop

I'm going to say exactly what I want to say we've got to get him out of there instead of just talking about it hurry.

Oh the trees in the cold oh we must hurry oh I'm running and the sharp stones etc. *it's not serious it doesn't matter it doesn't matter to me* the trees in the cold oh we must hurry oh I'm running and the sharp stones etc. *it's not serious it doesn't matter it doesn't matter to me.*

it doesn't matter to me
it doesn't matter to me

3.   **NIGHT WITHOUT MOON.**

```
        X  .  .  .  .  X
                        .
                        .
                        .
                        .
        X  .  .  .  .  .
        .
        .
        .
        .
        X
```

The next morning was like a Sunday (remember: The Days ***) a soft and luminous sensation with the light coming back into the house and the softness outside the sidewalk freshly washed by the sprinkler the coolness of the air mixed with sun *that's the kind of day I love* she'd always cry.

Ah just like me I replied and I sang:

> Hallelujah –
> snap
> the birds – click
> the wings
>
> pi-ii
> i-ii
> and it stopped
> pi-lii-liii
> and it started again

It's random – I told him – the stopping and starting of song but you'd never know it you'd say it's carefully arranged. Okay well that's just what I want to do it stops and it starts again and breaks up the time marvelously you can sit there and listen without doing a thing. Ah she said interested Ah Oh.

But on the island there was no one to tell this to and to enjoy things with (add here: My regrets) and there was nothing to do but to replay memories in your head and talk to yourself the rest of the time. Like Granny said in everything there's the good and the bad and she was right.

The skies change but not the soul Felix recited. Whatever you'd wanted to escape is precisely what you come back to. Intact.

5.   **HOW I GOT STUPID.**

I quickly gave up all regular work to free myself up for little idiotic games, reconstructions of banal scenes, conversations out loud, silly songs etc. There was a good chance I'd end believing them and that's just what happened.

The island: with the ocean as far as the eye can see with a little mountain in the center amid an absolutely virgin forest itself surrounded by cliffs with a strip of sand all around it.

Once I'd gotten settled thanks to the materials I'd found in the boxes recovered at the edge of the beach I needed nothing more but to: <u>one</u> survive and <u>two</u> escape.

In the forest I found a very tall and very straight tree (see: Trees, their essence) close to the stream that led down to the sea that I had to make into a canal in order to transport the tree. So all I had to do was to cut it up and drag it to the water and then let it float down to the beach where I could strip off the bark and hollow it out to make a sort of canoe.

Two questions: 1. would it require outriggers for balance? 2. would it need sails or oars or both? Answer: I decided to make a model of the boat in order to observe its behavior in miniature in a marsh or in a trough between the rocks to figure it out.

6.   **THE ISLAND, GENERALIZATIONS.**

The rocks stand out naked against the mountains. Some contain no traces of living beings, while others contain nothing but the corpses or fragments of corpses of animals or plants. Streams of water course across the ground and then plummet to astonishing depths. If you dig a well you find myriad skeletons of tiny animals all the way down.

Respiration is a phenomenon general to the island. The water that falls on the ground comes from the clouds. These, cooled by contact with the mountains, condense and drop the snow or rain that runs across the ground where it sinks in and resurfaces at the springs which run down to the sea, a part of which evaporates to form the clouds that are cooled by contact with the mountains and drop the rain.

A plant torn entire from the ground rapidly wilts because the quantity of water given off by vegetation is considerable. One hectare of field loses 1 million liters of water every four months. But during this time the plant must extract from the light everything that will make it nourishing to animals. Their carcasses will in turn be devoured by insects like dead branches and fallen leaves to give off various gasses which are inhaled in their turn. The meadow inhales its dead like the water that falls on the ground sinks in and resurfaces at the springs that run down to the sea, a part of which evaporates to form the clouds that are cooled by contact with the mountains and drop the rain.

Plants contain no traces of living beings. If you dig a hole you'll find animals at the very bottom that once dead produce a slow combustion which rises to the surface captures the already gaseous forms of the insects dead branches leaves or whole carcasses of abandoned animals the meadow inhaling its dead like the water that falls on the ground comes from the clouds which condense like the vegetation breathes and drops the snow or rain that runs along the ground where the water that sinks in mixes with the carcasses both entire and in fragments of swallowed animals or plants that breathing in their turn evaporate up to the surface where already dead branches leaves bodies fragments of insects disappear again like the water surging up from a spring runs down to the sea and evaporates to form the clouds which cool down in contact with the mountains and drop the rain.

7.   FIRST CRISIS.

Hello hello
wa-ke-u-up
it's morning it's morning

No uh what oh no

We'll sing you a little song *no I already said no too early no way too early no not moving I'm sleeping* listen let's not go through this again I'm suffering I'm sick *oooh I'm sick* oh that horrid little voice of yours!

The morning song
Theme: IT'S A BEAUTIFUL DAY ALL'S WELL IT'S PERFECT
I'm listening:

he cleared his throat authoritatively

Blue of the sky a kind
of cobalt and condensed
from a light blue like that
of an after rain the air
after rain the air
after rain the air

the air
no no blue

48

B-bird or blue
the the color blue
of the sky

That's it that's exactly it we're there. It's the X word, the X word that we were looking for <u>blue</u> blue of the blue sky.

Blu-u-e.

Just to help you out let me add: ferocity is an abstraction, speed and languor are abstractions, laziness and gaiety are abstractions.

I don't get it.

Okay so that means that blue or any other color is also an abstraction and that you must treat it as such if not you could say instead: it's beautiful or it's hot or something like that you follow me?

(...)

I'll skip the "Condensed from light blue" which isn't bad although around you it tends to seem a little complicated. As for the rest it's banal.

Time of the voice of forms of curves
of of pain of grief of fate of

Give up the ghost this little finally
yes and that means breath
respiration give up the ghost expire the lips

And what does that mean?

Give up the ghost this little finally
useless words example
ba-by the voice for speaking difficulty articulating sounds
baby infant clouds

?

Go away it's over finished I'm sleeping I've done nothing nothing I'm not waking up you're wrong.

WATCH OUT THE RIVER RUNS THIS WAY
the current is dangerous
the eddies
the silt
the-mo-ving-sa-nd-s
WATCH OUT LAWRENCE YOU'RE GOING TO FALL IN
no! come back
and hold on
to that branch
there
OH THE FOOL WHO LEANS OVER
watch out Lawrence you're going to fall in
come back up this way
this way hold on to me
okay slowly
okay
OH LOOK AT THE BIRD THAT
oh the wings oh he's blue brilliant blue
it's a bird that OH LOOK
oh he's going under the branches
there
under
there.

9.   **RECOVERED FROM THE EDGE OF THE BEACH.**

1. A box containing nails screws saws and all the tools necessary for carpentry.
2. A box containing tar ready for melting.
3. A box containing extra sails ropes and fishing gear.
4. A narrower box containing carbines.
5. A box containing some very beat up books including:
       a. A New Description of the Sir John Soame's Museum.
       b. Merwurdige Bemerkungen uber einen autobiographisch
          beschriebenen Fall von extreme Paranoia.
       c. The A.B.C. of Optics.
       d. Yellow blue Deep Blue Light Yellow, the complete poems of
          Mrs. ***.
6. A metal box containing a portable press ink rollers magnifying glass and

all the materials necessary for printing.
7. A wooden box containing a smaller metal box containing a series of let-
ters classified by date and person.

10.

You'll see that things go better if you manage to get organized
Organization my dear!
That's what makes the difference!
Songs songs that always works
fa-fa-fa-mi-do.

Note that in your case it's a total loss
all for the good cause
it's lost!
to make it work
it's got to rise a bit
yes.
A bit ideal a bit haughty,
a bit (...) *these are the branches the branches in the dark*

Ah that's it Ah no it's starting up again *the central black blot the blot a-
a central blot where the field and the night stretching out before it blot* **lis-
ten not now that that no listen that's enough no** *in the trees you see the
blot by the door you see the blot on the wall you see the blot in the hole you
see the blot by the door you see the blot*

Good [resigned], oh well what do you see in this blot?

*An an animal and at the same time uh the head of a man at the same time
you see the blot oh you see the blot the time the time of the approach of the
approach of d-death to arrive to divine one's end I've reached the end here
it is.*

*breath of wind of mist of smoke
worries shocks madness softness*

*smoke of mist or wind
shock of the enemy loving touching
of the body and of the voice
on on the body of his adversary*

after the body of his A of his A
after having touched one two touched

stop quit it stop

Summer the moon the hay the the sound of movingleaves
the soundsoundofmovingleaves

the sououndofmmmooovvvinglllleeaves

stop.

11.

The afternoon, when there's nothing to do when it's too hot or when the irri-
gation system is off or when it's raining or when the boat is aground when
the animals sleep (see: The sleep of birds) when there's nothing useful to do:
dry the fish, transport dry sand to spread around the room, gather dead wood
for the winter etc.– so, when there's nothing else to do: I close the windows
with the red curtains cut from the Lawrence's sails and rest stretched out in
the dark trying as hard as I can to control the voices oh oh the voices that

What?
Uh uh

Listen instead of just mumbling any old thing here's a model sentence:
1. Still and the years of a tree.
2. From one source from one point of departure and of time passed and what
is the age.
3. This tree this slender sleek shining black tree strip it.
4. And whose color is forest green meadow lemon yellow.
5. The ancient trees the green trees.

Do you feel the passage from these words to others?
The sense of coherence they impart?
The masses articulated to produce the general effect?
The clarity of your intelligence the images the force of contrasts?
The sincerity of the expression the intimate project the personal tone your
unique exclusive incomparable voice?

When he stops. Oh this

this horse-movement
of the hand

or slow down
its motion
Half-st. time. Ah!
stop oh stop the horse
pause

When he stops this horse
stop oh!
time oh slow down
oh of the hand slow down
oh!

Very good! very very good really right right that's just about it. It's too
personal detached arbitrary.
After all in the end what's left?
The final impression! Ffflled flown disappeared.
nothing
nothing
forgotten lost
and I need to know about what lasts AFTER
THOSE THINGS THAT LAST FOREVER.

12.   NIGHTMARES.

1. The most frequent: believing that the wall collapses getting up to hold it
up with every ounce of strength waking up and going back to sleep.
2. Rather frequent: believing that the floor dissolves jumping out of bed to
save it waking up and going back to sleep.
3. Frequent: believing that the boat is going to smash against the rocks get-
ting up running to the helm "watch out" not being able to stop it waking up
and going back to sleep.
4. Rather rare: believing that the fire gets out of hand running to the well for
water finding no water calling *Mister Robinson* running running waking up
and falling back to sleep.
5. Rare: believing that the boat breaks in two leaping up to grab on before
being swept away <to verify to repair> too late no waking up and not going
back to sleep right away.
6. Very rare: believing that someone is swept away by the waves or swal-

lowed up by a field of sound <here that's it carried away> a noise a voice an echo *Mister Robinson* minuscule voice carried away invisible too far away getting up to save it too late <already swallowed up disappeared> waking up abruptly and not being able to go back to sleep.

13.

So I go on ok but wait I can't stop myself from having words and I've got to get organized to note everything and to reorganize in memoriam so that this internal racket doesn't stop me from getting real things done.

Real things, good.
Real things so so in other words...............From where the genial idea the discovery (consider: Why I'm so clever) from the – the other – to work like Felix made me work. Exactly the same <u>critique everything do everything do it again</u> to absolutely master the unknown words.

To work like Felix to be in the library and to judge the relative importance of the books.

No doubt about it the stroke of genius was the song thing. What are you doing? Songs.

Go on then all right do your song then: the song.
then afterward you ask it's over? – Yep.

All right it's over
over over.
That's the rub: That's it, it's over?
Answer: Yes.
All right then it's over it's over.

But it's only over exactly when you decide it's over you and you alone.

ЛНІ ЛНІ ЛНІ ЛНІ ЛНІ
ЛНІ ЛНІ ЛНІ ЛНІ ЛНІ
ЛНІ ЛНІ ЛНІ ЛНІ ЛНІ
ЛНІ ЛНІ ЛНІ ЛНІ ЛНІ
ЛНІ ЛНІ ЛНІ ЛНІ ЛНІ
ЛНІ ЛНІ ЛНІ ЛНІ ЛНІ
ЛНІ ЛНІ ЛНІ ЛНІ ЛНІ
ЛНІ ЛНІ ЛНІ ЛНІ ЛНІ

15.

It's like this
and this will be like that but yes
read: I will tell you nothing about it
Good. And if not I hope it goes well me all is well
I'm so head in the clouds that I forgot
to send greetings to the blue dog
he must run in the summer,
that must be something to see.
Signed your –

I should add that the season was marvelous for all of us
and in u-n-ho-p-ed-for ways
we each did our part
so there you have it a good way to see things
you can't say that I'm not a good guy.
Affectionately.

Dear,
integral-warmth
thanks for the hat
I'll be able to be elegant this is hardly
the ideal place
but there are brief moments when it's allowed.
I'd like so much to make a model
something in wood or plastic
think about it
I've always been told that it's good for me.

Dear,
don't come without bringing you know what
the ***
one must not forget one's promises
to give is to give.
Me.

Dears,
Many thanks for the cruel festivities
we'll be eating cabbage that's clear enough
with the Chinese furniture
and all those ribbons
just close your eyes and you're there.

Dear,
the depths of the soul are indistinguishable from its powers
you can take it from me
if not same day same time.
The hand.

It's a fine day
it's a very fine day
yes it must be said: My Lord
you've seen me want to do you harm
if not you can no longer tell who's doing what.
Your servant.

God be praised I got the package
excellent the pigeon
and the sugared
it's the year that begins in fourth gear
as for the snow don't even mention it.
Snow.

Five o'clock is in full swing
Miss ***
wouldn't surprise me if
at the right moment
would give you the details
that just rang.
Soon.

No doubt these letters say more about it than the discussions I had wanted to hold at the time in order to really understand the situation. It's true that you only need to add them to the file as such to better understand both the suffering felt <u>and</u> the charm of the situation. One the suffering yes and two the nostalgia that I feel reading these documents. So in the same way the two feelings were blended. The same. The same these letters blend with memories.

– Do you like hazelnuts?
– Absolutely.
– And eggs?
– Also.
– and biscuits?
– Even more.
– You've got something in your pocket [very fast]
– ...Uh, n-no, nothing.
– Yes you do!
– Got NOTHING.
– Which do you prefer a big house or a little house?
– A big one.
– You said a little one!
– N-n...nothing...Ah!
– You lose [shouted]
– No!
– Oh yes that's it you lose!
– NO!
– All right! neither yes nor no—neither black nor white. That's all.

That's it Victory
won
for at least twenty minutes
hallelujah
it's barely believable promise
impossible to do better
on Sunday.

Dear old fellow,
this morning I pulled out all my (...)

one by one
interesting, no?
tell me, here we lack information most of all
Yours truly.
Read in the literature of gingerbread
– gingerbreadliterature –
I was told
that it's like that in the beginning
and after a change of diet.
Gooood moooorning Sir.

Dear,
don't forget
and even if it's not a real detention
I played in
1. David Recognized.
2. The Temple of Fortune.
3. The Imaginary Death.
yes yes
It gives off a retroactive radiance
this sudden glory, no?
Yours.

I swear to you that here everything marches in step
I am imprisoned
come get me if possible as soon as you can
please
Your devoted – fast.
[illegible word]

18.

An incredible mixture really I thought
shattered across the bed [aloud]
it's got to be cleared up

(...)

What made you laugh like that

nothing
(he makes faces and gesticulates)
nu-u-u-thing

Listen it's really very simple:

    1. I arrive on this island and purely for my own comfort I begin to talk out loud in order not to lose the power of speech.

    2. I consult old documents, letters, etc. to try to reclassify my memories.

    3. At the same time—and it's not easy—I try to do the work necessary for survival—food, shelter, defense and distractions—and it's no vacation if you consider the difficult position in which I find myself.

    4. I make as precise a record of it all as possible.

    5. At the same time I'm tempted by the most fantastic forms—it's my dada—and I try to integrate them into this project.

You understand then THAT IT IS I WHO SPEAKS HERE and not you. I am on this island I am on this island it's my island it's I it's my island it's my island I am there I am on it I am on my island.

19.   ROBINSON'S TELESCOPE.

200 meters

        a black rock
        a tree
        a fly

silent

300 meters

        black
        a silent fly
        material entity and yellow
silent

400 meters

        on the brown
        leaf

                            a black fly
silent

<mulberry-yellow>

A. fishing gear.

1. cane eight and a half feet long with two sprigs of bamboo attached (see:
Workshop, in Documents) & red and blue ligatures.
2. a fly collection made by my brother.

B. Action.

100 meters a rock and a good reservoir "no not there here **here** in this hole
here there all right still **here** very good"
the light slants across the water
do this <implies> there is a delicious way I thought charming fashion or
manner the vibrant air or folds deposits close to the branches foam divided
molecules under the water transparence *I understand nothing* I think while
speaking there you have it but no but no it's no big deal I don't take myself
for a fish
come back with me come back with me let's go yes
go back arm in arm—show me what you have in the basket

That's it show me the fish oh the fish oh
they're big oh they're big oh they're big

Eat 'em raw huh? [prancing around like a dog] *crack-crack*
All right already stop!
eat 'em raw eat 'em raw
[fake foaming to make it seem] Let's go oh

You just gotta talk to me like a dog
stop.

20.   DECEMBER.

In the morning I decided to drag the trunk to the edge of the water in order
to strip it and hollow it out into a canoe like the one I remembered having
seen in a book during the crossing.

Look at that pal
(that pitched and reeled in the cabin)

                                            wind black sea black clouds

Look at how, from a simple trunk, you can make a boat that
navigates   wind black sea
Fabulous!
reproductions with scale drawings

                                                    wind sea

                    Land (cried the lookout)
finally! Eh...fabulous!
Could you lend me this book?   **Crack**

at that very moment
                    Craaaack

The operation was difficult because the tree had to be dragged hundreds of
meters. The torrential rains had carved deep ruts that made it impossible to
use the system of rollers I'd devised. I had to haul it practically inch by inch
with a thick rope that I had in my stores and had not yet used.

The morning was gorgeous and the birds were singing in spite of the diffi-
culty of my work I couldn't help thinking that is was better to be here than
elsewhere—elsewhere, meaning back there—or nowhere.

Ain't we better off than nowhere?

Yes
—although
the

summer
—wind
yes

yes
—living
in

—in
the leaves
left— of a
disappeared

left
— in
the leaves

Who left? Who disappeared? It's always the same thing with you. Good Lord! Why can't you change your tune?

Felix, the first said, listen:

"Felix:—the word 'act' speaks of the body and the soul. For what does the body do when it acts? It moves.
Me:—It moves.
—Movements are therefore actions of the body, are they not? Some are reflexive, others are willed. I won't leave you to guess the rest, which you wouldn't like. And I don't expect to find in you that shameful foible that is the will or even anything approaching a semblance of motivity a vague desire to move even a little finger, in short—and he chuckled condescendingly *he is truly like us even if he is the tutor* in short, just as there are two types of action, the words that you employ—and employ is a grandiose term for the nonsense that you blither—can be divided into two main categories: <u>one</u> those that serve most precisely to cover a reality whose truth can be shared with the greatest number—I'm democratic by way of anti-idealism if you will *things exist outside of etc.* and all that rubbish—and <u>two</u> the other words that serve the whims of a single person and that is not tol-er-able [he screams] and get that into your little bird brain. It's distressing to have a head like that, you'll be decapitated one day, my friend, in the name of good taste. Your mother—poor woman— has told me how worried she is about you."

That's what he said. But now I'm going to talk to you about form. I'll give you an example; if you say:

> Dear,
> I'm looking forward to your arrival
> we'll fish in the water
> we'll eat grapes
> down by the well

To transform the thing you've got to start over from the beginning:

1. the summer
2. The well
3. The grape

The cool well among the leaves the dark and resonant pit = hedge tree dark interior of curved brick tile. The south red Tudor smell of moss (the cool well) the square cloister echoing circulating (see: The sound moving around in a spiral) enclosed space waterproof circulation = red light + grey + mint. Let it soak in the water (worn smooth washed in on the current) = water-lily leaves giddy insects fallen branches. In the water of what? Oh, yes, of the well (small garden wall green hummingbirds) Angels in the apple trees altitude of hats (?)

Which means?

(...)

I was busy getting the enormous trunk up onto a makeshift sawhorse in order to strip off the bark more easily when I realized it would be better to leave the bark on to protect the wood from decay. While I dithered around about this night fell. Black night without a sound. Nothing. The already familiar black night. Things lost in the dark <okay> come back voila.. Black expanses neither moon nor path by heart no opposing notions no obstacles no speech <okay> so come back. Night smooth as a lake without a ripple. Method: count one lake two lakes three lakes four lakes five lakes six lakes etc. And I'm asleep.

21. **MRS. JONES IN THE MIDDLE OF THE FIELDS.**

Tic tic tic
pom pom pom poom I hum

— I... I she shivered and swallowed a sob I
I shouldn't have done it
oh

— It's better this way?
— (...)
— It bothers you?

Crsss-crsss-crsss the cicadas

blue flowers that grow in the meadows
we're out in the middle of the fields

— Are the grass blades pricking you?

here touch
here touch
here

poplars poplars poplars

— I-I sobs
— Come on it's nothing I

poplars poplars poplars

full of
grace
full

— Oh...no I oh you know oh really...there
to kiss + to touch
and so on.

[ad lib.]

22.   DECEMBER (CONTINUED).

For a long time now I've been catching myself talking to myself. When I'm walking along the shore or when I'm sitting on the platform built high up in a tree observing the flight and songs of birds—I mumble hasty nasal phrases into my beard.

The pleasure I glean from this exercise made me decide to compose a series of little songs that I could sing from certain predetermined spots while knocking two stones together at regular intervals *This this horse-movement tack tack of the voice slow down tack tack slow down of the voice tack tack* and so on.

At first I recited these little poems slowly in a low voice but soon I was screaming the phrases as loud as I could and then the silence of the forest seemed even deeper to me (see: Resembling silence but even deeper).

This
this horse-
movement
of the hand

or slow down
its movement

pause
a
pause

hallelujah
clack
the birds motion of wings
clack
hallelujah clack
the wings
stop
slow down
the wings
clack

oh one moment slow down
me-bird
altitude
slope

halleluja
stop
fixed on high
there

It's I who decided it, I called out all day long. Me! I know how to do it! It's I who did it! *Oh that's great bravo* they cried *what luck*. But there was no one to hear and to tell me this. And I wasn't so sure I'd succeeded.

That's that I've exhausted my hatred.
And must one think it's irreparable if it's said
as one says "it's said it's said"
as soon as the bell rings: Dong! I'm not speaking to you anymore.

respond to that right away
Your—

Dear,
as to the subject of my (our) interest
express old pal: straight to the sky
and well sent! Ah they can say what they like
but it had to be considered.
Fondly yours.

I'm sending you the poem of the day
give me a <u>technical</u> appraisal please

        Pi, pi pi
        big big big blaaaack*
        galy-galy
        gaddy-ga-ddy*
        girlie-girlie

I'll explain.

*As in black, dark, opposed to light.

*Mama mama jonquil papa jonquil napkin (?) chicken bone cindered goose where
shall I go for a walk/where shall I go for a walk?

Friday.
Th' tel' me that the transmutation
Va-ge-ra-ma-ga-na (?)
it's directly real
From: va-ga-ga (to see)
to ia-na (way) there's nothing to be done
Like a sheet of white paper.

Dear friends,
the office is Ffffantastic.
Two green chairs

to say nothing of the windows
— with the Mrs. who shouts Goood
moorning Siiir
thrown in for free
Elizabethan no?

5:30	Rise.
6:00	Pray.
6:15	Study.
7:45	Breakfast and recreation.
8:15	Study and class
10:30	Mass.
11:00	Study.
13:00	Free.
14:00	The same thing in reverse.

Amen
if this goes on I'm going to end up believing
hail (...) full of etc.
Remember
in a state of pure battle
what is gained by one is precisely lost by the other
Result nil:
Zero-sum.

[In illegible blue pencil]
I am imprisoned
come get me quick
Felix and the others are dangerous
find a <u>fast</u> way
tell no one
urgent.
Alias Robinson.

24.   WHY THINGS HAVEN'T CHANGED.

In the clearing a little below the freshwater lake I had found yellow flowers
resembling carnations growing in abundance at the foot of a very tall tree
resembling a cedar but with darker leaves and lower branches.
I had made an herbal guide by gluing leaves and unusual flowers into the

unused pages of a large book I'd found in the boxes. I cut out the Latin names of the species they most resembled in order to find equivalents in form, color, or lineage between the species back there and the ones here.

It was morning oh and yes I wanted to make the most of it good legs good feet good eye swim run shoot walk.

Gooood Moooorning!
[I'm getting up I'm getting up]
Your dressing gown M'lord!
Sick! no it can't be true!
Ah I'm dying of laughter I'm suffocating

Black-blaaack-blackkk   Raspy voice with sniffles.

Lyrical.

Liquid that is at the level of that which contains it the water
darken flow disappear

The ground flooded with water the ground eroded washed away
deposited by the waters the mud is bottomless
after the rain

what gathers
Like certain cloth folds back on itself

tends to open up beyond
cloth
while they're very deep

(...)
A device beneath the skin
The air he exhales
                the luminous animal
but lighter for flight
action

Action of wings flapping   He mimes.
action of hands flapping
Wings movement movement of wings

What you're entirely missing is aim [I walked around the room with my arms crossed behind my back] yes! <u>it's about finding what's lost.</u>

And then on the metaphysical side it's NO.
What is really meant, for example, by "tends to open up beyond?"
It opens? It doesn't open? And why does it open and how etc. I WANT FACTS.

You mean disappointed? An opportunity missed? An object lost? Without recourse? Nothing more? Good-bye over finished? Is that it? Is that what you mean? Yes! All right
we've got to try something else.
We've got to try something else.

Silence. Clouds darken the sky the clouds have darkened the sky. Nothing more black. Birds turn in spirals along the wall the clouds have darkened the sky black silence. The clouds darken the sky. Wall. Motionless birds. Compact wind-swept silence. Black.

25.   TREES, THEIR ESSENCE.

1. Resembling a yew   but growing
                                   faster.

2. Resembling an oak   but less
                                   durable, with
                                   larger and
                                   darker
                                   leaves.

3. Resembling a poplar   but not as
                                   tall, with
                                   glossy leaves
                                   and edible
                                   fruit.

4. Resembling a lime   but with thicker
                                   leaves, a
                                   knottier and smaller
                                   trunk.

5. Resembling an elm   but with

higher
branches, red
roots and almost
transparent leaves.

26.

In the clearing, I found a small rise whose form suggested a tomb. In search-
ing around the base of this rise (remember: How I discovered the secret of
the island) I found an arm of stone dotted with spots of moss and blue mush-
rooms. I brought the stone arm back with me and decided to build a big box
in which I could put everything I found from then on.

He'd only had time to fill up a third of his journal during the crossing—and
anyway, I've barely read it because it's nothing but a series of boring nota-
tions June 22 / 54 degrees Fahrenheit / calm sea etc. And as I needed a note-
book in which to keep my own journal, I cut out the unused pages and
rebound them using the red sails of the LAWRENCE and glue I'd made by boil-
ing down the bones of a dead animal as I'd seen done in the book.

The work absorbed me so deeply that after a night spent drawing, I could no
longer get up in the morning as I'd planned to and I stayed stretched out on
my bed the entire day—and in my half-sleep I had the luck to be able to hold
on to the thread of my dreams.

DREAM

Croquet balls

                         red
                         yellow
                         green
               blue

roll
roll
through the wickets

how this tree grows its branches straight out (...) Wood that grows branches
or vines or ivy or flowers that unfurl the length of the trunk of a tree of a
shrub that spread out *like a kind of arm this tree grows its branches straight
out* cut a branch of oak of laurel of currant bush the branch broke under him
the bird leapt from branch to branch like going from one subject to another

not stopping at any one to get caught up in the useless details of a subject or to neglect the background to be in a state of uncertainty to be in the middle of his life

(...) not know what will become of one etc. To not know. To resort to every possible means to extract oneself from an awkward or dangerous situation is said of various things that have something in common with the branches of trees like the antlers of a stag like the branches of a tree to say the birds that perch in the branches of trees *the damp overtaking the grasses and the smell of water*

(...)
This tree of a green black substance fusible fish river? White bluish breaking fragile vault (...)

oh black night full of animals
oh black night full of animals

The memory of an action to abolish to cease to be in use to cease to disappear black yellow red green and to become these fields dust or wind this meadow this grass or twig or nothing.

This vegetation to become in its turn these animals partridges turtledoves their eyes their gaze fixed → to become in their turn **a field** to gaze fixedly who moves or trembles to draw something back with effort a spring the wind a cord a bow string a crossbow ff-ffff and already the traces are lost on the spot and already dead rotten decomposed to become this field in their turn **a field** leaves innumerable leaves.

Fruit leaves or flowers BIRD WATER STONE inscribed in the stone engraved underlined the damp overtakes the grass and the smell of water dead rotten decomposed ff-ffff the birds colored red green yellow turning *listen to me instead of sleeping* in the dark fixed here to become in their turn **a field a field** to stare fixedly who moves or trembles to draw something back with effort a spring the wind a cord a bowstring **a field** to stare fixedly who moves BIRD WATER STONE inscribed in the stone engraved *listen to me instead of sleeping* lost themselves in space these colored birds and already dead rotten decomposed **a field** to become this field in their turn leaves birds leaves here to become in their turn innumerable birds here innumerable here

(...) Their eyes their stares fixed to become **one**
to stare fixedly who moves or trembles

(...) and already the traces are lost in space and already dead
rotten decomposed
leaves leaves innumerable fruit leaves
in the stone
the damp takes over

To become **one**
who moves or trembles to draw back
—*to sleep*

in their turn leaves birds leaves here to become **one**
in their turn innumerable birds
to become here innumerable
here.

27.

Dear miss
infinite thanks for the two reproductions
of the bas-relief I've been looking for
I'm going to have them framed
in sky blue and grey wood
Oh thank you ever so much.

Already received:
a first case of books a case of paintings
and my machine will follow little by little
send everything
—the rest—

How are ze-childs?
This morning
it was a little bit nicer
we climbed up to (vertigo)
here we're all quite well
at the top up there we breathe.
It's beautiful.

There it is again
a letter much-ado-about-nothing
the true truth is that

since I arrived I don't think
I've exchanged 100 words
I groped around all night long
I listen to the water in the lake
lapping against the bank.

Dear Sir,
£220
+ 40
= £260.
And it ain't even magic.
No bitterness.

Read attentively your
<u>Eyes so delicate and an object so funereal</u>
we'll talk about the title another time.
It's very good except for this passage page 325:
after *If you'd seen what I dared to do*
DON'T SAY:
approached her and said softly
SAY: *I don't dare ask you for more.*
Cf. My previous dispatch.

[postcard]
This place is worth all the
Treatises on empty space
your–

Dear Mr.,
To clear things up
would you please explain as soon as possible:
1. Who in your establishment is in charge of that which interests me?
2. How competent is he or she?
3. Do you understand precisely what I expect of you?
Please reply by express mail.
Sincerely yours.

All right,
I'm continuing (...) with F.
ditto the evening
in the "blue room."
After a carbon copy
recopied variations of *lake Isle of Innisfree*

which gives you an idea
of the atmosphere.

[postcard]
the new studio is perfect
"Butterfly hunt"

Friday morning.
The Air-conditioned Nightmare is a great title
but someone's already got it.
In any case it doesn't go at all with
the content of your book.
It's gratuitous.
Affectionately yours.

P.s.
as for the documentation of the island
it'll take longer to get to it (the weight!)
In any case what do you want to do with it?
Quickly,
your—

28.

I thought I fell asleep on the edge of a cliff that the fire had reached my bed
that the floor was falling through or that I felt a weight on my chest or suf-
focation—an animal was trying to suffocate me or I saw someone sitting on
my bed next to me or standing in the room or like a black shadow on a
chair—however with the certainty that this person was flesh and blood and
that all I had to do was reach out to touch him.

I'd planned this room as a cell in memory of **—but I regretted no longer
being able to walk around the clipped square lawn and watch the walls and
the sky slowly file by or to observe the difference in color between the grass
and the interlocking bricks which formed the pathway around it.

All the same I had whitewashed the little cell-like room, which then looked
even more like its prototype—absence of the green desk and chairs—in
assembling the unfired bricks that I'd formed in small wooden forms and
then lined up along the beach to dry—I must say that this line-up so struck
me by its beauty that I forgot all my pressing problems—subsequently I

painted the resulting wall with a sort of milky chalk but this white-washing operation had to be repeated almost daily in order to keep the illusion intact.

5 h. Rise. Reading aloud, vocal exercises, throat stretching, crying sequence, rhythmic diction.
6 h. Breakfast while speaking out loud, technical advice, global reflections.
7 h. Whitewashing the walls while detailing the day's program.
8 h. Break. Unimportant thoughts. Reveries and little vocal reconstitutions of Class II memories (of minor importance with missing details).
9 h. Reading of letters. Packets chosen according to mood (see: Table of correspondences Moods/letters). Evocation of Class I memories.
10 h. Duet exercises and phonetic transcription.
11 h. Break. Nap, half-sleep, wake up singing.
12 h. Models of works in progress type I: alignments, ornamental irrigation, bird observatory. Repair the tape recorder, etc.
13 h. Models of works in progress type II: the boat, the bunker, etc.
13 h. to 18 h. Work in the fields, hunt, etc.
18 h. Reread the morning's transcriptions, corrections, additions, annexes, etc.
19 h. Take up morning's activities again (in order).

This small room looks out onto a large space like a courtyard but much more vast and with nothing that could arrest the gaze until it hits the sky. This view would allow me—if I were immobilized—to remain stretched out and to fix the patch of sky that remains—by closing my eyes—like a blue cut out in the dark.

DREAM

I had a nagging pain on my right side from an injury I'd gotten by knocking up against one of the masts during the shipwreck and during the first few months on the island I couldn't carry anything heavy (...) I had to construct a system of hoists and pulleys to transport the boxes I'd found from the beach to my provisional encampment *that's a lie you've got nothing it's all made up you didn't do a thing you're looking for excuses you're making it up* HOW I SUFFERED FROM THAT INJURY as it was very slow to heal I decided to cook *you didn't cook anything at all it's an absolute lie* TO COOK UP the large red grasses and to mix the resulting syrup with mud (...) to apply it to my shoulder to the motionless bones *what a genius what resourcefulness but where did you learn all that you liar absurd* BUT BEFORE LONG I'D REGAINED THE USE OF MY ARM AND RETURNED TO MY NORMAL ACTIVITIES.

The next day I thought:

No doubt this forced convalescence has made me deviate from my ideal program. Evil thoughts sprang up then disappeared then reappeared even faster: repetitive machine with two voices slightly out of sync accompanied by a rumbling that reminded me of the background noise I'd heard in ***.

This system was similar to the stone ornamentation that circled the central column of the dining room: three garlands spiraling up to the top (see: The Miraculous Song of the Birds).

The system takes on such scope and truth: the fire caught or the bed collapses—that's just it I think I see someone whose shadow grew oh resembling an animal the wall the wall that's just it caving in the floor gives way— I have to get up fast run to the window to breathe to get some fresh air to breathe.

29.

On the path **path path path** deep in the path deep of the forest in the deep forest **path in the forest** in the deep forest in the deep path of the forest path **path** deep **deep** in the forest in the paths **in the deep paths** in the deep forest the path in the forest.

Deep down under the water **the far grasses** the deep current **the grasses far** deep **under the water** the grasses the grasses deep the depth of the water **under the water** far the grasses **the current** far the grasses spiraling under the far water the grasses far deep.

This way yes watch out this way **watch out** yes follow me under here **watch out** yes there watch out this way follow me yes no this way **you've got it** this way there **watch out** below there yes **there** you've got it. No no watch out hang on there yes it's fragile therrrre yes below **no** here only here there **you've got it** that's it bravo finally that's it yes **yes** saved saved.

30.   MEMORIES IV.

Plac plac plac!?

– No really listen I have no desire to play.
– Ok ok, listen it's no big deal anyway you play very badly.

– Whose fault is that?
– Of course it's my fault yes besides everything is my fault but yes of course!
– Me, I learn things by heart I don't make anything up.
– Meaning that I do make things up?
– Yes!
– *I* make things up?
– Yes.
– So it was I who made up this game; I made up everything.
– You know perfectly well that I taught it to you.
– Ok now that's better!
– All right go ahead and think you did it if it makes you happy.
– You lost! You're supposed to say: "All right <u>poor thing</u> dream on etc."!
– Sorry, ok.
– Well and good that's it we'll stop because you've lost.
– Good.

Final commentary: game 1 badly played. 2 definitely mediocre. So, no tie-breaker *what no tie-breaker?* Nope that's it it's final <u>*there's got to be a tie-breaker*</u> no or else you pretended to cheat "the only way to tie" *no I cheated, period* anyway it didn't work anyway it didn't work. We're still alone.

31.

Pardon me
Dear
but now I'll be smart
now
I'm sending you
Mother, I

Dear father,
good good and congratulations I repeat
your son
to
think one for two
affectionately

Dear that you
dear father am most heartbroken today
isn't it, dear. No,
and thank you very much

and my best to *Mr. dog and the boy*

I'm doing well here
a few minutes on the beach
I stuck my head outdoors and saw the sea
good swimmer
and it was marvelous
baptism of fish.

6:30 up
go down to the courtyard for breakfast at 9.
[diagram]

Nothing special
Beg you you won't believe it
the least danger
never happens
nothing less than little dreadful incidents
a suffocating Inside
– sadness.

Shotgun shells
in an ex-terrain
why?
"it's dead" (sic)
Everyone has to say the same thing at the house.
Fondly yours.
your–

I hope
that you're doing well
almost everyone (alias me) is asleep

rise at 11:30
the infirmary
(but I'm not wounded)

Bread soup
more of the bread the soup & the bread
every day
free ration of fish and milk
for the ill.

"My word you?
<the boss> is he one?
<the boss says> "you've got to wash it in the sink which was full of plates
and all that"

So war's like that?
no no
I won't go back
I'll stay here, but
gotta choose right away
I said: I really want to.

<the boss>
It's not true
Where are you going?
<me> To the wood shop for the shavings
You're new?
Yessir.
right down the hall
you know <the boss> gotta mold 'em, etc.

A sign:
Eat slowly
Chew your food
fried sausage
powdered milk
aluminum bowl

A khaki uniform like that
lined in fur
I'll send you a photo of myself in uniform
most abstract
[diagram]
my horse got there first
(knock on wood).

Yesterday evening
sung
Oh *timeputupyourshuttersyoupropitioushours*
[softly]

Thursday,
threshold of death

this position [diagram]
oh misfortune misfortune etc.

The attached envelope

                           deaf and paralyzed
– Every person blind
[diagram]

Days pass
the electricity– the kind
a circular storm
perched in the best apple tree.

Under the west veranda
even without the bluebird
the bird bath is frozen
the bird bath is frozen
these are the good times.

~~My~~
~~my~~
~~dear~~
dears
Your–

The light seems (black)
– leap
straight toward the sky
of lukewarm air– the sky
Be it ever blessed with angels.

32.   **MARCH.**

Oh I see you're in perfect shape this morning.
silence
I'm sure you'll do this poem impeccably.
silence
Today I suggest the theme...
silence
Daring enjambments definitive line endings majestic beginnings.

to the branches of the branches
of the first tree that came
of the tree
of the tree

Squeaky voice

this torrent
this torrent this torrent
oh the oh the torrent
(refrain)

It's great, you've only got to add volume and breath thanks to an image. Example: Angel & Alliance. Angel & Alliance means those children's heads with wings that painters stick in their paintings and sculptors in their sculptures to indicate angels.

(...)

Get it?

(...)

Listen you're starting to get to me with your country bit. Always green, leaves etc. Nature. It's got to change.

I then explained to him that the cedars on the island resembled blue cedars but the trunks fatter and smoother the roots more shallow the leaves bristled on top and very cottony underneath and that the acorns were lighter green and firmer than the ones we had at *** and that that had nothing to do with it and that for inspiration we had to try to look at the truth even of things and not at their antiquated models from now on useless.

33.

MEMORY V.

In the garden

plac-plac-plac

– Uh oh!
– What?
– (...)
– Ok you start.
– No you!
– No you!

81

– Ok, I say: "Oh by what fatal misfortune do you enter here burdened pale disappointed disheveled tired."
– Pity me I'm only passing.
– No! You've got to say: "I'm only passing through and it's only by chance."
– I'm only passing through and it's only by chance.
– Ah finally here you are cloaked in your intangible secret!
– I'm nothing but a miraculously healed...uh...uh.
– HEALED FROM WHAT? How many times do I have to repeat it before you know the thing by heart?

– Try it again try it again [she pretends to cry]
go goodbye—it's already almost night and that's a good reason—goodbye it's night. Goodbye.

34.   MARCH (CONTINUED).

Night always came early on the island. I often let myself get caught by the absence of light. How many times I let myself get caught by the night—well so I'd have to sleep wherever I'd established my work-site during the day. It's impossible to return at night. As I knew I'd let myself get caught I'd foreseen abandoning the idea of returning at any price and of systematically staying at the spot where I'd begun working. Night always came early on the island *I've got something wrong in my chest* I'd let myself get caught by the light <something unknown> *I have a headache here it's burning me* how many times I let myself get caught by the night *I've got something wrong in my chest* well so I had to sleep on the spot my chest it's burning it's chronic they're going to operate right away I had to sleep right there they're going to analyze it *I've got something wrong here* I can't go back *I'm too sick* because I knew I'd let myself get caught oh well go to sleep right away: there <go to sleep oh please go to sleep> I am indebted to no one *I'm not saying a thing there is nothing I can say* I had hung my clothes way up high on a pole so that they'd find me *I'm not saying a thing* I won't come back for any price period. On the very spot: period.

35.   RULES.

1. Put your money on *blue star* odds are 36 to one.
2. *You're whose son?* (it's the time when the grass is so high that a horse and rider are completely hidden so the man-lion comes to see you—but he could

be disguised you've got to unmask him right away: you're whose son? If we don't find out: eat the excrement of the-un-recognized-beast in public).

3. $\dfrac{stand\ you}{I\ do}$ = I do (under)stand you.

4. *I look for* (...) folded up in little handkerchiefs I'm the one who's got it! etc.

5. *The Speaking Weapons.*

6. *That I like* teaching a useful number to the sages = π

7. *Sh'hhhh* which means leave.

8. *The game of royalty.*

9. *The dove* stabbed and the spurt of water.

10. *The key to the mystery* is determined by three cards drawn at random.

[title]

The Telemachus Case.

When he stops oh this
horse-movement
of the hand or slow down
slow down
his movement

Half-st pause ah
stop oh stop the horse
pause when he stops
this horse oh
slow down

When the horse stops
movement half-st pause stop
– stop
slow down of the hand oh
slow down

–

Stop-time
breath breathe out there
therefore movement
slow down there
slow down
Blue like that of the sky
– cobalt reduced
from a blue
like that of one after the sky
air

Stam the voice to speak
useless this
difficulty articulating sounds
difficult
example st-sta stands for?

If you move no
if you move from there
no
no more than a statue no pause
no

Watch out don't move no
pause it's over
pause
it's over

—

Breathe relax leg-
movement
held
one two relax

When he stops this horse-
movement slow down
– stop
so slow down
slow down

blue reduced
it's over example
– to stop
movement

After the sky
air

—

Articulated
clack
– end

wing-movement
horse
relax the air

The
The

—

I I feel strange things
this morning
yes really

What?

Didn't you say something? but I heard "uh"

there's something on this island how can I put it strange I don't know exact-
ly something that "hovers" you know up there

Nothing you're saying nothing so

Something that remains despite everything a feeling (because finally it's my
life "to be there") the fear of passing the time of life itself
The fear that it corresponds exactly *Ah that's my life*

Oh yes that figures
it's the complete time of your life that you pass

Good answer: ok (at first)

and second: but why [groaning] why isn't this a time "apart" a time for noth-
ing why? Get it: *it's like that.*

38.   WHY I'M EXCAVATING.

One morning I'd recovered the stone arm discovered earlier in the forest
(see: The Arm of Stone). Folded arm resembling the arm of a stone angel
covered in blue and green moss. You don't find a stone arm without finding
the rest pretty soon: religion? Corpse inversion? Ritual technique?

I'd prepared a museum for these objects: catacombs, anterooms, first room,
south passage, colonnade, second room, corridor, etc. You could sit down
behind a display window. You could see: stuffed birds, inscriptions, explana-
tory signs, the stone arm and other discoveries. You can conserve repair
ameliorate. It was the "museum spirit" that led me to restoring these things.
I had to repair them before displaying them specificite natura. Ex filia
paritem meminans quaelle patria. Sicut principem morituri sagitte. Utinam

vos et cujus indignes (must be punished) morituri (guilty of being dead) suspendis dies et caelus fuisse (suspended in the absent day?).

39.   **ANOTHER STRANGE DREAM.**

Mrs. Jones

Sir I'm so happy to see you
I'm certainly the happier of the two
(you might think he's the meanest of the three but
no it's not true)

the window is open
(the door is too)
the rays → the rays of light
clack of the doves

clack-clack

Sir I'm so happy to see you (he replies) I'm certainly the happier of the two.
Great! (he sings) what-gorgeous-weather

The next day
we went from one house to the next without finding anyone
Let them speak! I couldn't open the window
I cannot open the window
I cannot open the window

there'd be more fruit in our garden if there wasn't a wall here
I fall upon exactly what I need
you don't have to come here
good.

II.

The window is open
the door is too

Sir
I'm very happy to see you

I'm certainly the happier of the two

he arrived early and he closed all the windows

Maï dieur frennd, aï challe nevveur forguette youre kaïnndness and djènérosité

(I can't respond)

you are not woude you are notte stône'z
you are a mènne
mistir?

Mistir whoooo? She said checking me out from behind
her glasses
I wake up with a start.

40.

The island was furnished with immense forests whose resources seemed to me inexhaustible of wild game of all sorts of fruit of wood for building etc. But there weren't many meadows—stretches of open grassland fields lawns panoramic views—no and the sand began right at the edge of the forest. And that kept me from noticing admiring the differences in color of the fields depending on whether they were planted, plowed or in flower— grown tender green or yellow or blue or in fruit with the wind according to the rain etc.—no it didn't allow me see with the kind of detachment as if from the top of the *** Tower.

And if it's a nice morning fields meadows grasslands grown tender green yellow blue with fruit with wind according to the rain *this way Mr. Robinson* this way under there here here between the branches under grass high grass <slalom between the branches> stop she cries but here no impossible to have a view like that from the *** Tower.

This regret—and you know it's not the only one with tragic consequences (Granny always said the same things don't always have the same consequences and she was right with the sole reservation that "the same" in the phrase "the same things" means "belonging to the same class" and not "identical")—this regret made me decide to try grafting various plants and flowers to get some blood red and straw yellow peonies (remember: The peonies of Lady Peter W. Somerset).

The work kept me inside most of the winter in a hut made of bamboo and sheer cloth somewhat like a greenhouse where—with the aid of a scalpel and a clayish soil mixed with with a third part powder of flint— I tried to create these peonies. The result was something of a compromise resembling a kind of huge purple hortensia with spiny stems like those of a cactus.

It seems clear that I don't have a green thumb, and the idea was further complicated by the time factor. It's true that to honor things or their destinies or their memories it's best to propose something that can be executed <u>immediately</u>.

But the execution of what? It's true that to go around singing things like:

Who is this lo-st tra-vel-er?

just isn't enough.

41.

My dear,
Dawn or
If I were winter
<u>it's something</u>
I was thinking of the words we are today
what we were yesterday
the outside wall is wallpapered with leaves
your-brother.

August,
I did a little drawing based on a *Sunday morning*
pencil and ink
work in silence
lindens
– thorny hedge
lindens.

August continued.
Activity
glitches in the garden
turning turning around the hedge
turning around and again around the hedge.
I'm thinking firmly of you
at the origin ok above all I was deprived "soul"

and at the very most no one would be left
or a longer life
or all other advantage
or dark night nothing.

August continued,
I've got a workshop
with an arbor
exactly like the sketch above.
This letter is for you.

This summer I began to love S.
S, I love you more than myself.
she told me never, no, never
Never, no, never
how to do it
how not to do it.
The darkness got hotter and deeper
little dazzling
edge where the colorless
clouds
A.B.C. of drawing.

September,
Put a sky between the trees
not the local tone
blue
mixture of the afore-mentioned red and the afore-mentioned green
friend's advice

Day in a haystack
– turpentine
the dark line of the pines

colorless
is already speaking
your dear–

September continued,
if I do landscapes
there will always be figures so there
from here at least faster gone

I got
the rather good-box-of-colors
thanks
worked you up a canvas 20 x
in the open air orchard lilacs
colorless
is already speaking
no?

And that's all—nothing
the stature
unwavering repose

brain of flint
– small pear tree
expanse
of cold water and of air.

These letters were in the last packet in the box. It's true that I'm only interested in fragments
here. The complete thought of the writer being in the long run rather dull <*I must ask you again
to send me by express mail the following materials* (and then a list: so much of this and of that)
but if you can't do try to send me at least a quarter of it and if you can at least half (and then a
meaningless tirade on the low quality of available material) *if not I'll be in the garden* (and then
a discussion of the advantages of working in the garden follows/an anecdote of the Death's
Head Moth "to paint it you'd have to kill it") and I love working in the garden (then a sketch
with crosses and a legend follows: X: me; Y: the workshop wall; Z: the oleander; Z': the
view)>.

Acacias in the entrenched
cemetery the angel
trees so that
to see
– such tenderness

In the box I sent you'll find the reeds
things such as they are
with that I "But wait it's there that
and for the period in which she remains alive"
presence of mind in the words
change in the illness
don't forget.

September.
At the edge of the water
all the trembling
in this effect
lilacs

leaves falling
yellow

Very deep– the beach
with bushes
(dune)
blue bushes

nothing (not a book nothing
boules
and checkers)

morning
– like
dark-room

Here's sketch
of cypress a note
to type right

Rose
calyx plants
lightly
– a
pleasure.

Me
cerebrally

September.
heather
anguish
etc. I can't go live
with anyone no!
dead at bottom (cry)

A style
of rest of sleep
in the painting
living together

and you and I
workshop that will last
necessary at least useful to those who'd like to see
I shake your hand.

The end was an uninterrupted stream of complaints of whining and I don't have this and I don't have that *<but you know it's the current situation the market the trends and all>* you can picture the pose eyes up to heaven long sighs *<I've just got to have some hard cash>* the stretched-out starving bit *<hey* (startled) THE TRENDS (yelling)*>* and then more complaints *<I just can't get things straightened out* (sobbing) and then the opposite <I WAS THE ONE WHO DID THAT I WAS THE ONE WHO DID ALL THAT I WAS THE ONE WHO INVENTED IT I'M THE ONLY ONE WHO CAN DO IT RIGHT IT'S UP TO ME IT'S MY BUSINESS!> and you want to say: sure but of course fine fine you're right sure right just keep it up.

September.
try—a thin
sky

nothing
no problems

I've got so much to draw
such yellow wheat
its simplification
suggestive here

a style of rest or sleep
– presence of mind in words
change in the illness.
Truly yours.

42.   **WHY I BECAME AN ARTIST.**

Influenced by these literary people I decided to become an artist. Artist, o.k., yes! but how? No doubt the problems that I imagined at first were all the classic ones: how to represent the nature that surrounds me? How to render the shadow of a tree? How to render the shadow of a tree in a sun-lit field? And then: how to render the shadow of a tree in a sun-lit field with the sky reflecting the water which reflects in inverted color the field the way a wall can reflect a face? And I gave up.

How to represent dawn? How to represent dawn and its freshness the pure printed blue? How to represent dawn with its freshness the pure printed blue full of the strident singing of birds in flight the deep green hedges circling spiraling high ff-fff?

How to represent the pale line of the water and the line of grass? How to represent the pale line of the water and the line of aspirate undulating grasses articulated filaments? How to represent the pale line of the water and the line of aspirate undulating grasses articulated filaments?

How to represent the line of the grasses in the rapid freezing current running rapidly? How to represent the pale line of the water and the line of aspirate undulating grasses articulated filaments in the rapid freezing current running rapidly with the reflection of the pure imprinted blue sky with the strident singing of birds in flight the deep green hedges circling spiraling high ff-fff?

43.

and between the hedges **incarnatus est** between the hedges the car glides **et incarnatus est et spiritu** between the high green dense hedges **et spiritu sancto** between the hedges **et passus et passus** between the hedges **et resurrexit**

et passus et passus between the fields the car glides and silently **et passus** glides **et passus** and disappears **et passus** glides shadow the car **et passus** and there **et resurrexit** right there **passus passus** there **et resurrexit**

pa-ssus serious **pa-ssus** acute **et passus** together **passus** still serious serious and acute **passus** together still acute and together serious and acute oh **et passus** still a voice and here **et resurrexit** now **et resurrexit**

the car the car low between the hedges **et passus** oh below glides hidden **et passus** the engine shifting gears **et passus** full bore spiral between the hedges **et passus** the engine between the hedges **et passus** shifting gears oh and finally resurrexit **et resurrexit.**

Under a tree, I'd constructed a lean-to made of planks under which I'd put a table and a hammock which let me come work in the summer across from the main canal running down to the lake while at the same time keeping an eye on the fishing lines dropped at the precise point where the fresh water met the salt water and supported a variety of white eel whose young I captured and raised.

More sky
more rain
I stayed there to watch then to work to survey the canal which ran in a sort of ring around the tree the water spiraling and I could see the fish turning around the lines.

And I closed my eyes
I no longer saw either branches or sky
and I could stay there
to watch + to work.

In the evening I had to continue mapping the island—precursor to the three-dimensional model— using cross-hatchings spaced in inverse relation to the slope equal to a quarter of the distance between two consecutive curves as I'd learned to do at ***.

As I was drawing, I realized that I was becoming more and more contemplative. And that's why today I am a saint—right before that I wasn't a saint—today <u>Just like that I'm a saint.</u> St. X. decides to become a saint (we'll call him St. X. from now on) A saint? Yep. But how? How'd he do it?

X became a saint through boredom, through sheer laziness, but that's still "why he became a saint" not "how."

And since when? It's well known that if you set out to measure a rough coastline you'd better know where to stop or you'll end up having to consider the angle of every stone and the position of every grain of sand.

THE SAINT

In my cell to write—reread—consult—on a platform something like a house raised to the height of—with high windows on the space containing—the lion poised on the flagstones—the peacock on hold and the partridge dazed—birds striating the windows above—pale day around—me living in a pocket of ingenious wood—as if set up in an office—writing inside a desk—thinking in the drawers—dark all around—the lion in the background gamboling over the flagstones. The partridge dazed and the peacock on hold.

45. MAP.

...this way... and there watch out turn right... yes and there the second left that's it... getting closer... good... path... good... here... here that's it...THERE.

NO it's this way... it's exactly the opposite... what?... No... it's never been there... never never... you're wrong THERE'S WHAT UP AHEAD? A (...)? NO NO not there you're confused

... what do you mean "you're sure"?... NO NO it isn't there no no... never IT'S NEVER BEEN THERE ... no.

What?... YES IT'S HERE... yes just a little way... you turn there... you only have to think of it... in reverse OH YEAH... it's funny like sometimes... don't thank me. NO IT'S NOT THERE AT ALL... you're wrong... uh no that's gone the... what?... no no you'd be better off to... THIS WAY AND THEN STRAIGHT AHEAD... exit there that's it the exit... yes this way... that's it.

46. MAY.

No doubt about it everything returns to dust said Granny and she was right. All these words committed to paper they'll all become dust—these discussions all these pseudo-dialogues all these early morning and late night thoughts—it's all going to turn to dust gone over evaporated life's nothing but a storm of thorns etc.

You can see here that the approaching end forced me to give up my earlier work in preference to more productive pastimes out in nature as they established a link with that which surrounded me. Like Felix said, go a little deeper and life's nothing but a storm of thorns etc.

I'd constructed a platform in order to watch the birds closer to the sky between the branches. I noted everything I thought necessary date hour and precise musical score and then I went back.

Monday	piii-riii	piii-lii
Tuesday	patiiii pattt patiii	pat
Wednesday	piii-ta-ti	pirriii-pirii
Thursday	i-i-i	patiiipatiii
Friday	/	idem
Saturday	takatakatsss	patiiii pattt
Sunday	pat-piriiii	/

47.

The **white** birds the birds the **white** birds in the high the highest branches **the white birds the birds** the white birds in the highest branches on high **then disappearing** all around then coming back.

the white wings of the white birds in the highest green branches **the white wings** in the wind the white wings in the highest green branches on high **the highest** the birds.

The white birds the birds the white birds in the high the highest branches **the white** birds on high then disappearing all around then **coming back.**

the white wings the white birds in the highest green branches the white wings in the wind the white wings ah **in the highest green branches** the birds.

48.   **VERY OLD MEMORY II.**

Would you like to see
what else is in your bag?

                    no/
                    box/box

You'd like to see if there's anything in my bag that interests you no/
box/box (inferred it's not a bag it's a box).

Oh
(S. watches them disappear
S. gesturing "gone")
Gone. All gone.   more/
                                  gone/

Go on he watches them disappear S. imitates the "departure" go! let's go let's go oh still/gone.
Oh still gone: TEARS.

What is it?
(S. trying to pull horse out of box)
Mommy help?

> no/
> horse/
> Mommy/help/

What's going on? S. tries to pull the horse out. And you need Mommy? No/Horse/Oh Mommy
help me.

> Boom/

Boom. Uh oh what happened?
what happened? S. laughing pointing to the horse on floor
> Oh/

You're silly today
(S. laughing)

> Oh/

Boom/boom. Oh there! what! what's going on? what's going on? she laughs she points to the
horse on the floor on the ground. Oh/you're so calm today what's happening? (she laughs) Oh.

baby eat/baby eat cookies
baby eat cookies
Mommy open?

> Mommy/
> open/Mommy open

What is the box can you open it?
can you open it?
Box. Well, Mommy's gonna see what's in it
Ooh.
(S. looks inside)
More?

> more/
> more/

More?
That's all there are
More? I don't SEE any more.
No
I look for more animals

> more/
> dada/

99

Baby eats/baby eats cake etc. Mommy open? Mommy open Mommy open etc. And so what's in the box then huh? You can open it, good. And Mommy etc. Ooh (S. looks inside) more? More/more/more? That's all! THERE ARE NO MORE. No. I look then I search I want more animals. Search. More/dada.

Horse
(S. putting horse on chair)
                                        there/
(S. having trouble getting horse
on chair) I'll help. Okay, M. I'll help you
no room for horse
                                        over there/
Help?
over there?
(S. places horse)
There it is!
(S. taking horse from chair)

Horse S. puts it on the chair here. S. has trouble holding the horse. I'll help yes. That's it yes I'll help. No place for the horse here here/Hey! help please. Here. S. puts the horse back. That's it! S. takes the horse from the chair take it/Take it. Take it.

                                        back/
Back. Back.
(S. putting it on floor)
                                        down!
Down.
(S. stands horse on floor)
                                        uh oh/there
Uh.

Take take take the horse! S. puts the horse on the ground. Down on the ground down/Down. S. stands it up. Go on oh/go on/down.

49.   X. AND ME.

Yes. It's enough to repeat exactly what you heard. Why not recopy what you want to say instead of complaining. Take back what is said. It's enough to repeat exactly what you heard. That's just what I was trying to get X. to understand. This X. has got to do better. X. could make a little progress. X. has a soul.

It's enough therefore to repeat exactly what you know. The fullness of spirit that means in all circumstances you're playing with all your faculties... the round and square space where a stairway ends... the movement of a liquid that alternately rises and falls... the adjective that describes a surface composed of rounded folds...the coal dust that collects in the bottom of a bag.

If I take the place I am now... okay... a surface... let's say so many miles square... by... the total amount of reclaimed water in inches per year... given by year... taking the rain into account... more than a thousand gallons per second... just mark it on a graph... calculate the frequency... record all the numbers.

What you get with frogs <a series of repeated croaks> and already I no longer saw the lines in the water—eye glazed and troubled—

And night came and I heard the giant frogs <a series of repeated croaks> and I no longer saw the lines in the water. And I fell asleep. Then a dream deep night already seen. Nothing.
Not nothing nor the sky
black water

Oh
liquid that (...)
sleep
is (...)
patient (...) that
that can't end is
this that can'

patient (...) that
that can't
this that can'

50.   NIGHT.

I dreamed of the forest where I'd been that morning but larger darker and even more unknown. And I discovered a statue buried under a pile of leaves and dirt whose finger pointed toward a huge tree at the foot of which was buried a small metal box that I couldn't open.
12345678910 The combination? Impossible! and I woke up with a start

Sleep
is patient (...) that
that can't end is
that which can'

no this that
or this
oh but oh you
oh—
I
speak what
that to say that

this that can'
this that cannot—

black
more nothing
black.

51.

The love he brought her was huge and dangerous
The love he brought her was huge and dangerous

The l-ove he br-ou-ght h-er w-as hu-ge and

It was storming outside rain wind

come-there
touch and kiss

here + like that + that

gust of wind through the pines

                                        and she was content
and she laughed
Ah!

More nothing
swirling through the night
sleep
bad words
anguish

to be more precise
storms
weather or tumultuous

that turns to a torrent
painful as thinking
of a cliff

sleep
stops me
my survival like stocking up
alone
black shadow

middle of
flesh and blood
no one
no one
stretching out an arm

of wings
of the birds
the sleep
deeply

to move
the leaf
fins of fish
freely

turn in the dark
such awaited

touched
– central
angels
the blue the speed

of children
in their paintings
to represent

dust & wings
the air ff-fff
as calmly as possible

m
ove the leaf
f
ins of fish

f
reely
the d
ifference

d
ust & wings
the air
f
ff-fff
the calmest

t
ouched
-
central

angels
m
iddle of
flesh

n
o one
stretching out an ar

Each morning that the weather was nice—that the morning was cool I dressed to make a tour of the island. The birds sang high up on their branches (note here: How I imitate the songs of the birds)—the giant ferns the enormous yews—I inscribed or engraved messages at various foreseen places.

I've been here for a long time signed R.

I am here [in stone]

In memoriam

A WALK TAKEN BY A. AND B. ON 8 JULY
20 MILES
DEPARTURE LAT. 567. LONG. 610

In memoriam

A WALK TAKEN BY M. AND H. ON 7 MAY
35 MILES
DEPARTURE LAT. 561 LONG. 680

A.C. — *Ante Christum.* Before. Things ancient or vanished. Ex: *No, I did that before.*

A.M. — *Ante Meridiem.* Before-noon, Morningish. Up-early. All there is to do. More generally is said of all positive thought.

Arbor. — All that touches on the education and the incorporation of the surrounding nature. By extension characterizes all self-examination.

B. — *Barred.* That which I never said. Lie or approximation. Erratum. Ex: ~~The love I brought her was huge and dangerous~~. I never thought or said anything of the sort.

B.D. — *Bachelor of Divinity.* Exiled.

B.H. — *Body Heat.* What I'm looking for in Mrs. Jones.

D.Uncert. — *Date Uncertain.* That which I can no longer find again in spite of my classification. Said more generally of everything non-classifiable but important.

Ext. — *Exterior.* That which is outside and by extension: that of which I'm not quite sure.

*** — *Family of ***.* Said of the entire human *** group or all individual acts that can be attributed to any one of them.

H. — *Hapax* or *Isolated Attestation.* That which happened to me only once. Word pronounced a single time. That which I said one time and will never say again. By extension is said of all promises.

Ib. — *Ibidem.* In the same book. Is said when one thing resembles another to the point that the two are confused.

I.T.P. — *In The Park.* Out of line or out of the game. Said in the case of a blunder (unforeseen) or a fault (premeditated).

L.M.W.W. — *Line Made While Walking.* Characterizes all reflexive activity. Ex. *reading while thinking about it.* Said of art in general.

M.S.R. — *Members are requested to keep Silence in this Room.* Complete silence is required in this place. Same use as *Total Disappearance.*

Passé. — *Passé.* Something understandable but no longer used. A persistent but unimportant memory.

P.M. — *Post Meridiem.* After-noon. Of the evening. Characterizes all nocturnal memories.

P.S. — *Post-scriptum.* What I write you afterward. What I still have to say to you. More generally: Why I'm attached to you.

Q.V.	*Quod vide.* See this. Method of accelerating artificial thoughts.
R.F.	*Robinson File.*
Rt Hon.	*The Right Honorable.* Felix's title. Is used more generally for all unknown persons.
S.L.I.	*Superior Level Inspiration.* Is said out loud within a commentary on the transcription of bird song. Can also be written in the margin of such commentary.
T.D.	*Total Disappearance.* Phrase to say immediately in case of vocal doubling.
T.O.	*Turn Over.* Turn the page. Go forward. Is said out loud to give something up. Variante: †.
TT.MM.SS.HH.	*Their Most Serene Highnesses.* Imaginary nobility. Highest possible level of a thing. Is used more generally to demonstrate extreme approbation.
T.U.G.O.M.E.	*The Ultimate Goal Of My Efforts.*
Viz.	*Videlicet.* Clearly. What I really want to say.
X.	*X.* Is said of all things or persons unknown but useful for demonstration purposes.
Yd.	*Yard.* All measurement. Replaces all numbers. Ex: *this bird is Yard away.*
Z.S.	*Zero-Sum.* Equals zero. Final result of all operations. Sum of all things.

55.   WHY I RETURNED TO MY CHILDHOOD.

Second model of the boat: larger than the first but smaller than the last—just barely large enough to stand up in or to pose a monkey or a mannequin in. I knew I'd be able to navigate it along the canal down to the sea using a triangular sail made from the red sails of L. + held by a rope.

The boat—me lying flat in the bottom level with the passing water
between the grasses
at the height of the buttercups daisies reeds
the slight
current
rippling

the boat gliding out beyond the grasses of the small canal

pull with the rope to jostle the landscape

the boat alone moving forward
small tide
—alone.

56.

According to certain archives the Robinson system is a very elaborate tech-
nique of automatic, autonomous, and perpetual doubling. All information
processed by this system is multiplied into parallel and irreconcilable series.
For example if I say "a blade of green grass"

1. a a blade
2. a blade of grass a blade of green grass
3. a blade of green green grass green grass
4. a blade blade of grass
5. green green
etc.
and the green—after a while—becomes independent of the grass and the one
can never find the other again. Like this island is separate from me and each
word spoken out loud takes on an existence independent of the context in
which it was spoken. And *ad vitam*. Result zero. Sum equals nil.

A system of automatic isolation. One One system of isolation one/two auto-
matic a system of isolation a system of automatic isolation.
Automatic.

A system of isolation A system of automatic isolation. A system a system of
automatic isolation a a blade a blade of grass a blade of green grass a blade
of green green grass green a blade blade of green green grass

Automatic isolation. A A system of isolation one/two automatic system of
isolation a system system of isolation one/two I've been here a long time
signed R.

I've been here a long time signed R. I've been here a long time signed R. a
blade a blade of grass a blade of green grass a blade of green green grass of
green grass a blade blade of green green grass.

TO
YOU ALL THE FRIENDS FAMILY & OTHERS DISAPPEARED
ETERNAL REGRETS.

TO X.
UNKNOWN FRIEND IMPOSSIBLE TO FIND AGAIN
TEARS.

TO THE
ASHES
OF THOSE WHO REMAIN ON HIGH
JULY AUGUST SEPTEMBER
THINK OF YOU.

AHHHHH
I MISS YOU SO MUCH
TAKEN FROM THEIRS BEFORE THEIR TIME
CENTURY-WITHOUT-YOU.

HIS YOURS MINE
PARTED FOREVER
AND EVER AND EVER
YOURS.

HERE
THE SACRED AND RECOVERED
BONES OF THE ONE
BY WHOM WAS
EXCLUSIVELY
HERE.

ASHES AND FINGERS
ON US
& SHINE.
SO BE IT
AND INDEFINITELY CALM
CENTRAL
AMONG BEAUTIFUL THINGS.

58.

Like the thunder and the sea that you hear or all other sound that comes to show that everything is in everything—all sound indicating that everything is in everything. In the same way I must do the same thing with the inaudible words that accompany a normal conversation.

It's enough to precisely retrace what was happening being careful not to omit or add things here and there. The pure truth. Even a religion wouldn't have invented such a crazy thing. As if I said: I'm Robinson! X. is a saint! I'm X! etc.

At first I was defeated by insignificant conversations such as: "How are you Mrs. Ramplee-Smith?"

So it's enough to
FLY-BZZ FLY-BZZ.

So it's enough to say:

How's it going Mrs. Jones?
How's it like yeah goin' Mrs. uh Jo-ones?
How's it **how** uh yeah like goin' Mizzzezzz Jo-ones?

Hoooww zzit **how** uh goin' Mizzzzzzezz
Uh meeezzzzuhzz **Djo**-Jo-nes meeezzzzuhzz wat?

Hhouuzzit **how** yeah uh **Whaa** Mizzzezzz
Uh meeezzzzuhzz **Djo**-Jo-nes meeezzzzuhzz wat?
Hw hw?

hey! hwzitgoan djones?

This was the last phrase I brutally remembered, like you wake up with a start when you realize you're sleeping.
And I found myself back at square one. In a single stroke.

60.

And it's like this it's there **it's the light** it's the emotion of **the hands** the magic the magic took it the magic took it **like this the light so soft and like this.**

Between the hands seem seem to me **appear to me nothing** now nothing appeared cold appear **cold sad** it was however the only **the only thing remaining** the small the small end of things **loud voices** empty gesture the **piece** the cold piece.

Took took the hands the hands vestige of year **vestige of year that surrounds the same** the same silence light **so soft and this way** fled within solid beginning of everything **integral beginning.**

I have them I have them **they seem to me useless useless nothing sad** white field long sky long sky like a kind of **I threw them threw them away** these useless thoughts.

Fled into the solid **gone into the hard days** gone into liquid time **swallowed up in days to come** entirely into **without return without their returning without thinking of it** gone engaged in days to come.

Abandoned to what he has to say abandoned to **everything that there is to say.** Return of **return of these beautiful days** known **known days the waters streami. morning polish** smell of morning water **return of these beautiful days.**

Ash yew ash **of morning** abandoned to **what I had tried to say abandoned to the complete night** black dark **today but nothing [] today.**

The simple image evokes nothing but [] we come to the end we always come to the end of what I have to say **I'd need another life to do it** it's too long.

Then was it that this luminous thing **luminous** idea of **simple image** evokes nothing but **we come to the end we always come to the end.**

The heterogeneous days I have them I have them **they seem to me useless useless nothing** sad the heterogeneous days **like we come to the end of all I've understood up to now** the sum total of what I've understood **me entire party of things** entirely **engaged in days to come** solid time **before.**

Fled into the **solid left** into the hard days **left into fluid** time swallowed **in days to come** entirely into **without return without its returning without thinking of it.**

Return of these **return of these beautiful days known** days known **the waters streami. morning polish smell of morning water** return of **these**

beautiful days fine line of with **before narrow** time just before.

I have I have the most urgent the essential the essential I have at the moment now **there it is I have the most urgent** now **he knows he he**.

It it **how it thin thin this thin membrane** that it is thin this division **nothing not even nothing not even confiding** not a word **not foreseen nothing**.

Why with it the inside the ins. **the inside so warm** with her **I miss the time** I told her I need another life **an entire life** to regret a life **to regret that**.

He sits her down he lays her out to glide along the side **lies back slowly** lies back to hear the **miraculous** the miraculous **interior sound of the living**.

In front of the [] **In front of the []** and the [] the tre. **the white field of flight** the white field of bir. **the green striped [] of bir. birds risen before**.

I have them I have them **they seem to me useless useless nothing sad** all these actions all that I've done **I've thrown them thrown them all away**.

Give it back to me it's my only souvenir **I don't have anything but it's the only photogr.** the only **there's** only **that** between the hands seemed cold **the pieces** fly fly off across.

The rest disappeared I didn't even want to burn them **no the only side to take where did these pieces come from there from what horror** it's I it's I.

Here we are ent. enter **sit down** cold **excuse me** excuse me I **it's a regret it's a regret that to** she with she the int. **the the miraculous interior** it's my stor. **do you think me so stupid as to have not already understood so as to not know** with a comic gravity he said that **with a comic gravity** I already got it.

Already floating all absent **floating** he sits her down he lays her out **lies back the two hands the neck already floating** unstable **unstable** she seemed to him smaller **already smaller than she is** than she is in reality **her voice very small**.

The neck already floating unstable **unstable** she seemed to him smaller **already smaller than she is** than she is in reality **her voice very small**.

From where is detached alone with precis. she detaches herself alone with precision multiple thought **almost detatch. almost entire alone naked** precision with a frightening precis. **her legs around her long legs her arms.**

She gre. **she grew at bottom** at bottom alone naked naked **from where detached alone** with precis. she detached herself alone with precision frightening thoug. **almost detach. almost entire alone naked** her legs around her long legs **her arms.**

In back folded the neck **the neck in a small fold** of the neck thin fold of the neck of the int. **the interior so warm of her** to beat.

In front of the [] **in front of []** bir. **birds already risen before** whiten **white leaving** to beat close **to wings.**

It doesn't move it does **not move** I I fear **don't dare there no on her no that not alone.**

Type of **lie** her trouble no the **the rest alt. the rest disappeared** I didn't even want to burn them **no the only part to take what did the pieces break off of** the of what horror **it's I it's I.**

Give it back to me it's my only souvenir **I don't have anything but it's the only photogr.** the only there's only that in the hands seemed cold **the pieces** fly fly off across.

Return of these return of these beautiful days known **days known** waters streami. **morning polish** smell of morning water **return of these beautiful days so I'm saved.**

Before the bir. the open field or the bir. **the open field where the already risen bird** the white field of white wings.

luminous **but to have alas all that has already been said in front of** freed from all that has been said **abandoned to what he has to say** abandoned into all **that there is to say.**

Isolated within what there is to say **indifferent to future** I'd need another life for **a whole other life for that so I'm saved.**

Everything that moves is mine it's the **it's said that** was it then that **is that the cause of it all** is it for that that **all that is tomorrow is mine.**

Remains **black** remains of **sun-lit field in front capable** capable of lasting of **surviving under any condition but it's not that.**

I'm capable of capable of surviving under any condition **but it's not that no** I'd need a lifetime **an entire lifetime** to say it but I don't have the time **it's not that.**

Abandoned to what remains to be said it's better the forgotten words I throw them away the **capable of surviving under any condition** I toss it away they seem **useless sad** I'd need another life for the **say heterogeneous days** I don't have the time.

All that is tomorrow is mine it's better **it's better complete time in days ahead** the days ahead carried off into the **solid of everything that remains to be done** so I threw them away the others **thrown away left** they seemed **sad cold useless.**

The sum total of what remains **what remains to be done do you think me stupid enough not to know** what remains the **to do the sum total ahead.**

Give it back to me it's my only souvenir **I don't have anything but it's the only photogr.** the only **there's only that in the hands** seemed cold the **the pieces fly fly off across** seemed cold the **give it back to me it's my only souvenir** seemed cold **all that is tomorrow is mine it's better** seemed cold.

The Return

He's late (he knew he would be and claims he missed the train) but given the importance of the preceding session I don't mind waiting.

When he comes in he tells me *that he has nothing to say that he hasn't dreamed that there's nothing important to say, that it doesn't count* (I explain to him the meaning of the expression "to count on" and "to count as someone" in the sense of: having value).

Him: *And if I've got nothing to say what good is having an appointment.*

Me: Everything's fine. Just relax, that's it, like that.

Him: *Like this, cross my legs?* (he crosses his legs twice)

Me: No, no, don't cross your legs (I uncross his legs almost by force as if he were paralyzed (1.).

1. I have to do this at the beginning of every session. Often it's his legs but sometimes it's his arms or he can't lay his head down on the couch *I can't lay my head down* or if he needs to write something to show his real handwriting or to draw he claims he can't hold a pen anymore *I don't have the strength to hold the pen* this operation completed, he's usually calmer and the session can begin.

Him: *I take off my shoes?*

Me: No no you're fine like that.

Him: *So* (he becomes confident again), *what have I said so far?*

Me: That you weren't on this island...that you've never been there (I consult my notes) that it's all a pure fiction, that you haven't done anything, etc.

Him: *Wait a minute I never said that no no no. What do you mean I said I was never on the island?*

Me: You were the one who said it.

Him: *Wait a minute remember I'm only here because I want to be, not because I have to.* I could have not come, right?

Me: But yes of course 1.

1. To get any results, I have to let him think he's coming on his own. In addition, I always leave the door open so he can hear the sounds of the house. I ask my daughter to walk in unannounced from time to time with banal questions. Are we going to eat soon? Are we going for a walk along the lake tomorrow? Haven't I seen the cat, etc. I, myself, interrupt the session with remarks like: my but I'm hungry! or isn't it a beautiful day! I've gotten into the habit of taking rather telegraphic notes (preferring their speed) of his essential statements trying to reproduce the tones and stresses which are very important in his case (see: The Sonorous Aspect of Recovery). I've no doubt that without the diligent typing of Mrs. Jones, I could never have managed this work whose true importance I didn't recognize until today (see: The Robinson File).

Him: *Besides, you're rather nice to me. I come to see you because, finally, I understand myself better with you. I'm going to tell you a little something; you're pretty smart. You make interpretations, which are not entirely without truth.*

Me: Thanks.

Him: *You really are rather nice to me.*

Me: Thanks.

Him: *So, I said I'd never been on that island?*

Me: Yes, last time.

Him: *Wait a minute up to now it's been me that things happen to **you're not going to start telling me what I did and didn't do** that's a bit much you know. It's up to me to decide what's true and what's false.*

Me: Absolutely.

Him: *Listen I'm not feeling very well how about if we try again tomorrow?*

Me: Sure sure I understand.

Him: *Tomorrow then* (he rises gathers his things and leaves without another word).

2.

2.   **TEST.**

50 cm.

Guts by which my soul cherishes yours alone—be it forever our consolation. Oh I've many things in my heart to say I don't know if I can put them down on paper. I thought of you throughout my long

80 cm.

thought in you throughout my long journey home, I say grandly. Your three wishes for mortal life don't displease me because they're just, as long as they're not bigger than their objects

1 m.

merit. No doubt it's quite right to want life for someone who's given you the means to conduct your own—but my dear there are a hundred yes Ah there are infinite yes

1.25 m.

I'd say infinite ways to guide you without that: it's he who guides you hold your heart high stay there don't move no

1.50 m.

high, bind it indissolubly to the will of this very good heart***

2 m.

Mr. Robinson read this quickly read

121

quickly this Mr. Robinson watch out stop trap here here

3.   JUNE.

If I go to see him, it's by choice. Therefore, two possibilities. One: we understand each other. Heading toward change: yes; an explanation like "to count on someone": yes; the possibility of telling all in great detail: yes. Going over it again to get a clearer idea of where it's headed: yes. Two: we don't understand each other. No explanations: no. No change to hope for: no. No coherent version of the thing: no.

I returned to the same spot back to the window, white walls, chairs, etc. Daughter comes back in: *we're going to give you the the...Oh oh but what have you done?* Me, I laugh. Good, good, she goes to find the mop. Meanwhile I open the window and climb out onto the ledge. *But where are you?* Oh oh she panics you gotta see it (I see it from behind the shutters) *but-where-is-he?* (thinking it's a game) goes to look under the bed in the cupboards, etc. finds me at the window *he's crazy* she says *but really sir why are you doing this?* the life of infamous men I thought and yet neither long hair nor black nails. Come here I tell her you're very cute. She grabs me by the hand I leap into the room and I fall on top of her *oh no* blouse, etc.

At 5 o'clock on the dot hour of winter birds dive into the green bushes and twitter around for a half an hour and suddenly silence. Close the curtains.

Soup and biscuits. Gruel-to-chew. The already-said the already done *why don't you want it it's good* it goes on like that (pushing away the plate) cars going by below roaring sirens jets of water rain muffled cries screams.

It swells the mixture, it thickens, it weighs on things *but sir* the young girl continues (I'm going to skin you alive I am) *so read the book you like so much* she gets excited you gotta see it *the book the book where is the book?* (hidden under the pillow you idiot) *here it is I have it The Complete Life of Mr. Robinson* (laughing riotously) good I'll read it out loud: "The singing of the birds awoke me with a start! the flock of birds spiraling high" *it's beautiful it's the beginning I like best* keep quiet a minute if you want to hear what happens next.

"The flock of birds sweeps upward in a high spiral at the edge of the cliffs the sound reverberates against the natural wall" *why natural?* Wait he's comparing it to a courtyard...closed making it resemble an aviary *how's that?* a natural wall because natural you see like not constructed *hm Ah!* she says *but it's not a courtyard if it's a wall!* Four walls in a square equals a courtyard equals an aviary—if there are birds inside, of course—*Ah* come here approach blouse click white buttocks and wine stains hair in staggered rows.

The darkened part of the window. The light wind rustles classically through the trees. Sleep my beautiful friend sleep, etc. It changes nothing. Not a breath of air nothing. Black night black rolling through the dark muffled under shadow nothing not a breath.

4.   **THE ROBINSON FILE. THE TALE.**

The sun shines
open your eyes Charles
eat your bread
the flour is made of wheat
the wheat grows in the fields
the grass grows in the fields
children don't eat grass.

But where's Charles?
he's nowhere to be found
where's Charles?
don't move stop breathing
Ah there he is!
come here Charles.

Come and give a kiss
Charles has to come when he's called
Charles,
no Charles **no.**

Go Charles let's go across field

there goes a knight
he goes fast
and he's already out of sight.
Charles is tired
poor Charles
let's go back to the house
the ink is black and the shoes are black
the paper is white
it's winter it's snowing
throw some snow on the fire
see Charles it's only water.

Oh no it's dirty
it's too dirty
go on it's spring
it's raining
look at how it rains
does Charles know how to swim?
no
if Charles goes into the water he'll drown.

Bring me the teapot
the tea is too hot you've got to wait a little bit
no children don't cry
Charles don't cry
this child isn't Charles.

Night falls
bring me a candle
blow out the candle
close the curtains
no don't close the curtains
Oh moon
it's night it's cold
there are holes in the ice
watch out Charles
the sky is black.

Charles does not have wings
Charles is not a bird
Charles has hands birds don't have hands
birds don't have teeth
fish have no legs

they don't walk watch how they swim
Charles couldn't live under the river
Charles is not a fish.

Charles is not a fish.
Charles is not a fish.

There was a child but it isn't Charles
he doesn't know how to read
Charles knows how to read
IT'S A BEAUTIFUL DAY
Get up come along
come outside noon it's time Charles.

Look at the sun
turn towards the sun
it's south
the other direction it's north.

Look at the black clouds Charles
birds eat seeds
people eat everything
go come let's go back to the house
look at your shadow behind you
it grows when you walk.

Look at your shadow behind you
it grows when you walk
no Charles the sun doesn't touch the fields
we're in the house
sit down Charles.

Charles you mustn't go out into the fields alone
you could get lost
and night will come and you'll be lost
and you stretch out in the grass
Charles you're so tired
Charles it's night
now
and it's a terrible story to tell.

There it is Charles we're at sea
the sea is not a river

Charles is not a fish
the wind blows the fields are far away
the fields are far away the wind blows
go Charles come on
go Charles come on.

5.

He comes back in without a word he sits down and begins.

– Yeah right where was I? Oh! yeah, at the beginning it seems I was invited to ***.

– You mean to say that maybe you weren't invited?

*– Oh no that's crazy. **I tell you it's my house** and the fact that they changed the whole place later is secondary (1) but I had the right of passage no? (2) And* <u>for life</u>.

1. See: The transformation—how a house becomes a correctional facility then again becomes a private dwelling. In the plans you'll find the precise explanation of these changes, which so profoundly affected his psyche. His anxiety is above all geographic, an acute awareness of modifications of space: *The man of the islands* or *the Robinson*—except that there's no Friday, no friend, all alone, etc.—I'd written in a preliminary study left unfinished for lack of background material.

2. <u>The right of passage</u> it was through expressions of this sort that I realized that his thoughts were much more complex than I'd first thought. Standard expressions, juridical scientific or grammatical stereotypes, citations *at the time I said (it was said) right of passage (but I think no less of it), etc.* You'll see that the story of the island conceals a great number of such phenomenon (see: Sickness of Style). It's also true that I had to consult various appendices (see: The Robinson File) to be sure of certain points. Moreover it was during this session that I grasped the miraculous connection between the main story he told and the official documents, reports, testimonies whose veracity can now no longer be doubted.

– What right of passage?

– That's getting mean. It's exactly like the story: "Above all if you have a question don't be ashamed to raise your hand" me I understood nothing and I never raised my hand yes yes (crazy laughter)

and I was proud of it.

– (he hums)
　　　　　　　　　him her them
　　　　　　　　　the sky is grand and the cherry trees too
　　　　　　　　　Vrr. (moving his arms) *Vrr.*

6.　　　　　　　　　　　　**THE ROBINSON FILE: TRANSCRIPTION.**

The Queen

[the court is a square of courtesans]

Oh but †
whisper clamor muffled cries

well that's it
well that's it

the queen is †
the queen is no longer Madame oh
of the cave → of the towers black flags

WE NEED A REPLACEMENT
who?

enormous armor plumes, etc.]
......well all right I suggest Mrs. Jones?
– Mrs. Jones? AH AH AH But she's much too young! impossible no

hold on I propose .... rezdsgijulez illsaecareilo (I can't quite catch the
name) yes yes miresaligabiier particilaforise danlamezur (I don't catch
any of it) What?

– It's him he cries
they leap on me

I wake up with a start.

7.

Dear Sir,

I the undersigned (...) as a member of his family alert you to THE REAL DANGER that you run in establishing any contact with him (alias you know who).

Right away we saw THE REAL DANGER HE REPRESENTS and I can give you <u>written evidence</u> (please find attached this evidence). What I've written here has been read and countersigned by the rest of the family and <u>intimate friends</u> who have all drawn the same conclusions as I. YOU MUST NOT TRY TO DEAL WITH HIM. I have put drafts of these documents at your disposal to prove it. [illegible word]

8.

the grrrrass
is grrrreen under the brrranches
the frrrrog is hopppping through the grrrrass
oh caaaaatch it caaaaatch it

Chorus:
the frrrrrog
is hoppppping
in the grrrrass
sooooo caaaaatch it

caaaaatch it!
achhhh (piano) achhhh (pedal) achh
derr dokktorr isst -t demmmm lannnn'd
Hiiiiimmel, etc.
The doctor isn't there so tough luck for you
Hiiiimmmmmel, etc. the doctor isn't there
touch luck for you
caaaaatch it!

9.

Several days later.

Him:– *I have to make a coffin for a dog. I don't have the time it's a rather large coffin (for a wolfhound) man-size (doubled over) about 3,543 cm x 4 √ 87 = ∞. Not counting the density of the wood. Giving it approximately in planks: in white pine let's say huh. Yeah, the dog: sudden edema of the leg (very rare) they cried over the dog you should've seen it.*

He was so intelligent that you would have said that he cried with them! (he was called Fox no... Burt... Rak... Luk).

But I don't have the time seeing as this coffin isn't the usual. ± 5 cm is standard up to that size (way too large even if the body is doubled over) What? No, no. I don't have time because of the dog. I have to make a coffin for a dog (1).

1. *Time to eat!* What? Okay, I'm coming! (someone's calling me) for example: that's what I call verbal contamination. The thing is how to get something out of it. My friend Michael calls it "the calligrammatic temptation." All right I'll give you that much I told him the other day. You're wrong etc. The tree is hiding the forest etc. What he doesn't get is that in the present case the coffin-for-a dog, it's not a laughing matter, it's a way of thinking etc. (follows an exchange of letters etc.).

I have to make a coffin for a dog.
[ad lib.]

MEMBERS
are requested to keep
SILENCE in the room
By order of ***.

11.

Several days later.

– You know when you get to that state how can I put it—well, material ecstasy—because there's nothing to interrupt the marvelous flow of sensations memories or... (he gets up and walks off with his hands behind his back and turns around speaking in a low voice and comes back and sits down)

The wife-of-speech-has-an animal body but oh ain't that the question (turning and pointing his finger at me) *what body **an animal body?** and why huh?* **What tenderness?** *And for whom? And who is tender?* **And who loves?**

All right okay so I believe excusively in....—oh yeah so it happens uh—to the degree that it reveals the... (he rises) *and uh the ecstasy the touch of grace hallelujah-click the birds in the sculpted air surrounding the thing... stopped in flight... tears!*

Hallelujah 1. (shrill voice)

1. I didn't intervene knowing that something new was going to happen. And in fact, the appearance of this second voice confirmed my hypothesis: it assimilates the shrill voice *the tiny voice* with another character—and he's capable of distinguishing it from the one he calls *the responders* by crying *no it's a fake.* The case is definitely the most complicated one I've ever known—to the point that I think his name will become the name of a whole new complex. My friend Professor Michael Lawrence helped me enormously with his advice, his precision, and above all his memory of case histories, that science that consists of rooting ideas in the context of their appearance. Michael was the first to propose—in response to my written questions—the category of "Illness of style," and I'd like to give him my warm thanks here. I'd like also to thank Mrs. Jones for her devotion "her gift of second sight"! in deciphering the often rather illegible documents that I handed over to her. True, such an extensive project can't be accomplished without a thorough understanding of its context and, I must say, without a peaceful setting in which to work; I must also thank my wife and children for that. I'd also like to mention that I was aided by a very precise working method. I built a sort of lectern in my office that had folding shelves that allowed me to juxtapose several texts and thus study them together. In the adjoining room, I installed a small couch, which allowed me to lie down during the sessions and thus concentrate more fully on the voices themselves. It happened that often other sounds, such as those from the street, voices, passing cars, the sounds of the apartment: children crying, doors slamming, furniture being moved, muffled

laughter, and the sounds from the courtyard: singing birds, dishes clattering, etc. would blend with the words of my patient. The combination was sometimes miraculous in the sense that it's often the context that holds the truth and that gives interest to the repeated words (see: The Repeated Words). A red window shade gave the whole room an orange tint, no single object arrested my gaze, which made me think of W.'s Seminar; I believe it was this reassuring thought that gave me the courage to follow the project through to the end.

Hallelujah
click
Movement
movement of wings

– Did you talk to yourself?

– *Yes and no, I don't know if you can understand that. Like Granny used to say: I don't mean speaking from a desire, which is a separate passion and is related to the future, but from an agreement by which one considers oneself from that moment on as connected with the object of one's love: so that one senses an all of which one feels oneself only a part and of which* **the love object** *is another. And I can tell you she was right* (he leaned back emitting little joyous cries). *Tears, tears. Sculpted, yep.*
fleep....fleep....fleep

(moving his finger in a spiral).

12.

Go back into the room. Shut in. Sleep hard. Tucked in bed. Birds enchanted with sleep. Pretending. *Oh oh Sir it's time to hiiiiiii*—she slips on the oil that I'd intentionally spilled in front of the door—oh there there my sweet what happened the floor's too slick! are you all right? Are you hurt? *Ouuch!* here? *No. Ouuuuch!* here? *No.* Here? *Yes.*

Go back into the room switch the bed with the table table in front of the window chair at an angle carpet pulled up fresh paint tsk tsk *here you are sir your newspaper if you'd like sir I can open the curtains* her hands are all over everything she's touching all my things *if you plug the radio in with the extension cord here the music* (she raises

132

her eyes to heaven) *the music!* three four no that's a glitch that one listen for the fourth beat there yes! and rééé mi mi ré fourth beat there there yes done) she sits down. *Any news?*

Read this: two guys in a cave they'd got all ready for it kidnaped three women. Cut off their legs, medical torture. Stripped the bones and stuck them under glass for observation (calculating the degree of suffering etc.). Decay etc. They caught them by the smell *it's horrible* come here *it scares me* no no it's nothing *why do you tell me these horrible things?* Come here! *here?* Yes.

Listen to this <she comes forward> a guy thinks it's still the war and hides himself on an island. He trains every day for combat (?) gone crazy. They find him practically fossilized on an observation platform in the woods. They find a whole bunch of things etc. *but that's horrible* not so bad as all that *oh if I find* come here (blushing) come <you're gonna see what you're gonna see> *oh I want you to you* <red known lips breast> *oh it's you oh it's you* yes.

13.

He comes in and before even sitting down:

– *Over the erased tracks of S.* (strident voice)
– Why erased?
– *(...)*
– Who's S.
– *Nothing on S.*
– *Over the erased tracks of S.,* is that a title? What is it?
– *Don't count on it.*
– Why?
– *Listen* (he gets worked up) *I love S. I really love S. so I'd like it if you'd please a-voi-eeed talking about her, okay?*
– Okay.
– *<Over the erased tracks of S.> I love S. I love S.*
– Why this island? (I go back to the beginning)
– *I take great pleasure in talking to you.*
– Why this island?
– *(...)*
– But you didn't really leave?
– *I leave why? Well to prove that it's a mistake the notion of a sub-*

133

lime education, of progress-in-things. You've got to have counter-project with a purely scientific aim.
– What do you mean by scientific?
– *Ask me some more questions? Is it you who asks the questions?*
– I'm the one who asks the questions. What do you mean by scientific?
– *I'm glad you asked me that. All right well there are the birds. I took it into my head to devote myself to them completely: nest-building, songs, habits, tastes, loves (mating rituals, family protection systems, etc.). Thus, this voyage which was above all <u>research</u> before the catastrophe you've heard about, the shipwreck etc. and the system of songs.*
– The system of songs?
– *That, that's the childhood of the art* (he paused for a long time, staring fixedly at the ground) *and so...you follow a bird. Observation and then... you do what he does and in the same way... no. No I'm making that up, the bird thing that's a lie.*
– Why do you tell lies?
—*BBBut but what's this at first it was nothing* (he howls) *and now there's all this! all these problems oh la la.* (1).

1. *Now there are all these problems* this phrase came back to me the next night. O.k., there's no cure possible. There's nothing to be done. I get up and say to myself: <u>there is no cure possible</u>. Why? Well because it's beyond hope. Irreversible grief as in an irreversible coma. Crossed over to the other side, elsewhere, postmortem, outside. Tremblings, fixed stare, pupil fluttering like a butterfly (see: Final resemblances) flapping of wings, click-over. Can't even move now, can't get up or speak. Definitive. Are you sure? Yes. Cut a little bit out to see if it helps? No. Going to leave him like that? Yes. He is I and I am he. No difference. Together to the end. Same. The duo, the last.

14.   AUGUST.

Mr. Robinson? Yesssss... I say it so softly that the girl can't hear *Mr. Robinson?* (a pause) *It's Mrs. Jones, can I come in?* (I locked the door knock knock *Mr. Robinson?* Nothing. Don't want them to come back and force the door (I open it and say nothing) suspense.

Tap tap tap there they are. Hello I say casually <he'd locked the door, they say> *it's he* she cried. The boss thought about it......................
.... *Tell me, my friend* (I'm suspicious)

you've got a fever, show me. I give him a swift kick in the stomach. <Oooof> doubled over. *You're crazy* she screams. So they grab me.

Put to sleep early. Window barred. Black night always a little earlier. Put off until tomorrow what you should have done today. Sun getting bigger. Meadow end of field. Sun growing in living memory. Natal grey. Goes back before the beginning. Soft speech of before. Clarity of everything.

Wisteria-wisteria edge of the rippling stream. Bzz the flies Bzz the flies. Motion of the grasses. Subterranean fish. Mud-tunnel. Fish fins. Gills-speed. Backwards clouds.

To remember the root of every thought. Opened shutters closed windows open distant sounds to come back in the dark—cries of children groaning-calls. Stretched out in dim room groping sounds. Vegetative-last-bough. Pollen of nothing in the total black..

Mr. Robinson? Yesssss... come in. <the crucial moment> *How are you doing this morning?* Oh all right (whiny voice) *Open your mouth and stick out your tongue. Oh but it's all white* n-no. Pretending <don't move play dead> ***Oh Mr. Robinson?*** OOH! scared huh? Come here! *Why?* Come here I want to tell you a secret. Hands + fingers + lips.

15.

– You seem to be doing well this morning.
– *(...)*
– If you'd like to tell me something before we get started, feel free.
– *Well, I wrote a little something.*
– Something important?
– *No, not at all not at all not at all.*
– I'd very much like to know what it is.
– *I know... I know. All right, you can see it. The story of... it's astonishing, no? Everyone tries for the emotional tone. Not me. It's over isn't it?*
– It's over.

He rises and picks up a thick file and says out loud:
– *It has to do with a series of non-classifiable items and if it doesn't*

work you can interrupt me (he blushes) *these are just working notes,*
what counts is...is
– Read it, afterwards we'll see.

FAMILY RESEMBLANCE *I.*   *I coach him as to tone*

The first objects
of a deep sleep
of a blue sky—   *Cut! and there just after:*
the statue

Which leaves:
The first objects of a deep sleep
of a blue sky
                    the statue   *Ah! the statue-sky (backed up against) etc.*
  Birds and the top   *That's a beautiful image, isn't it?*

                                                     and it goes on

Branches of these beautiful trees

                                                     and it ends like that

FAMILY RESEMBLANCE *II.*
                                                  It's an arranged dream
The contrary the reverse the verso
Me, I came back (without his knowing) and then him all of a sudden
on
word for word he says

he says: "Sir," him (all of a sudden)
"Sir,
          Gallop? (...)
On a horse
On a horse
and there in the dust
oh! right away at a gallop   *in the dust*

And me: "Sir"
I say "just one more question if you will"
and I listen between the trees
to cry out   *I want to know more*
"There you are there you are" and my tears
stopped halfway in falling.

136

– There you are.
– It's very beautiful it's very interesting.
– Yes, it's my life in images, get it? It's a particular tone. Of course it's not like in five minutes you can...
– Of course.

FAMILY RESEMBLANCE III.

The the winged monsters
stupor ***
first words
rou-rou rou-rou

Who, on the point of dying
Above, burned
– the birds?

the legs the thighs the arms missing
(in a jar?)

– It's...more abstract, it seems
– But what are you talking about? What despair do they mean? WHEN DO I GET TO TALK? Answer me! (1).

(1) I look at him without saying a word saying nothing showing nothing, as I always do, as it's my job to do, as I was taught to do, as I have to do. I say nothing, I wait. It's like that.

– What despair do they mean? WHEN DO I GET TO TALK? But do you know what it's like to never get to something de-fi-ni-tiv-ly accept-able. No "This isn't enough, that isn't enough" and on and on. And you, what are you going to do about you? What's the cure FOR YOU?

He sits down takes a paper from his pocket and reads:
It was a Thursday. And Thursday was the day fixed for building the boat. I'd brought the tree trunk down by the stream-come-canal that led to the sea. This done, I dragged it across the dry sand in order to strip it and hollow it out. Next I had to fill it with water then with large hot stones in order to enlarge the opening. But it was impossible to cut through the bark because the tools I'd found in the boxes on the beach were in such bad shape: the saws chipped and the scissors without handles. I decided to give up the work and to use the trunk for firewood and to go back to the house to work out a new plan of escape.

– Where'd you get that one?

– IT HAPPENED TO ME. That how it was, it's true. How can I put it (he rises and walks around the room like a lunatic) *without without... verbs, nothing interesting... I've already explained the importance of the action... the verb... I'll add that in certain cases it indicates the passage into a state... or the manner of being: this child dreams, or a production: the apple tree flowered and that the word action must be understood in its largest sense.*

– No no, my question is: where ever did you find such a story?

– I'll start again. The verb is a word that expresses an action done by or done to the subject. If I say "the wall leans," the verb "leans" indicates the state of the subject; if I say that "the light is," the verb "is" indicates the existence of the subject. Get it?
– Yes, absolutely, you're right (at this point I realized that I'd gone too far).

– The verb is like a mechanism, eh, The Celestial Voice, the...the machine (he gets worked up) *producing the voice that... that you don't know... no—that you know but of which... you understand nothing* **Onononorororonono** *that you know by heart and whose meaning you understand....without grasping it. It's what you know best.*

It's what you know best.
(very shrill)

(very low voice) *does that bother you?*

– Calm down.

(he leaps on me)

END OF MANUSCRIPT.

17.   **CRACK-CRACK IT'S OVER.**

A motion

– You're quick, young man.
– *And mean,* I said. *Quick and mean.*
– And mean as well. I take back what I said.

– Why're you here?
– *An accident.*
– (...)
– *What?* I say. *I...*
– That's it. Just go right on down and they'll take care of you.

Talk to the other guy.
– Put him in 23.

He leaves me alone for a moment then comes back with a billy-club

– I'll take care of you.

[ad lib.]

18.   **SEPTEMBER.**

Journal of inventions. Sum total of all I know how to do. To build and then make technological notes (the mistakes the attempts and the things to be learned). What one can do.

The Garden-of-the-Institution. Virgin at the bottom in the rockery. Little pathway with benches. And each time the old woman who wants to kiss me. 1. avoid the dandelions in the lawn (don't walk on them) 2. climb the wall 3. jump onto the branch 4. slide free into the field beyond.

YOU DON'T HAVE THE RIGHT TO GO INTO THE FAR FIELDS. Interior Regulations. Add up all the excuses that offer access. Consider why and how to go. Consider interest, consider my actual capacity for going.

YOU DON'T HAVE THE RIGHT TO GO INTO THE FAR FIELDS. Which is to say: field of dandelions going there equals not coming back. Night of the spirit said Felix. State the right to not do it—this said during the weekly meeting. *This meeting gives you the chance to say what's on your mind.*

Make note of the stupidities and learn them in order to recite them in another voice. Go back into room night of the spirit you speak. Go to sleep thinking about it. *Hey Mister! Mister Robinson* <there he is go fer th'other idiot> *Ro-bin-son Robinson de-ear* <I don't respond>

I hide under the bed. She comes in she wants she wants (other earlier useless thoughts)—"SUCH STORIES!" I think under the bed—keep still she'll hear you heart beating etc. DON'T MOVE th-thump th-thump *Ro-bin-son?*

Searches everywhere thinks it's a game (I see her legs from below) searches for me doesn't find me goes away turns out the light—silence.

All this for nothing. I've already seen all that stupid story of the island. False machination, sum total of all I know how to do stuck on a pin. Regrets, eternal regrets. I'll tell all at the next session, etc.

Routine night with nothing to do. Night without view. Light wind. Frogs and the murmur of waves coming up to the window. First drifting into sleep half-dream half-machine. Night sweats. Cot. Saddle. Pig's foot. Pig of milk. Milk of cow cow in pasture pasture in fields fields in pasture pasture in pasture pastured in pasture peace in fields peace in peace.

19.

Divine morning and no shadow on the painting. Make spoken jour-
nal. Inaugurate new more efficient manner. Don't screech but recite
in a low even voice. To the ear. With an eye-dropper and for internal
use only.

(spoken)

Yes, now it's the birds
[brother & sister]

became birds
now so high

branch-machines
fixed
vertical-song

You can't talk to them any more
now
who says?
alias-birds
speaking
to the sky

"you're lucky"
said Mrs. Y.
you lead a charmed life

to have them all the time
over your head
no?

The leaves. Oh. Green.

I reply:
they
have NOW become birds

so they're <u>inaccessible</u>
to you

What d'you mean?

They're birds
yes—entirely
in beloved trees

Ah!
ah but I can't talk to them any more
ah but I can't talk to them any more

No.
body in flight
vowels in the beak
drawings in the air
implied: it's not for you

So I write the following
message on the wall:
ex-terrestrials
the sign
R.O.B.I.N.S.O.N.

the mind calm
Go back house
quiet thoughts
thoughts toward those already flown
quiet thoughts toward those already flown

REASONING

brother-bird
sister-bird
trajectory of heights
point of the garden

cedar-to-cedar

needles in the sky
zebra-love
never alone

not hidden cloud
not under the leaves

together
neither mud
nor ashes

Definitive
—path-sound
perpetual

CODA

Thus and so: they have <become birds> thus they are "in the sky." If they're in the air, how to join them? How? <u>At each session</u> I was told: No you can't do it. But I never said that I wanted to <become bird> become a bird. No I said join them join them in thought: I'm with you that's all. To fly together. Navigate the heights. Indistinct small head body light bone-feather cage of wind thorax-singer.

I am a thinker-bird with you. Futile discussion on branches. To fly together. Hallelujah. No tight throat no tears light air and warm the huge bouquets of bound leaves suspended.

So if they've <become birds> send permanent signal: bip bip point bip point. Thought-machine. Wing-movement.

Before (see: My life on the island) everything came back to every-thing. No gap between things. The "classic manner." That's all over *Oh uh Mr. Robinson what's all this?* <wracked by tears> *but what? We've lost heart but you're going to leave soon it'll be over* the mourning of everything nothing to do black choked heart *Mr. Robinson?* And she—disappearing minuscule foot of the bed vacil-lating lamp little black treasure tiny soft words disappeared choked heart night <like> forest night nothing night night.

20.   NOVEMBER.

They come in. I hear them <here they are> *Mr. Robinson* <in falset-to> they've come for the result. Tap tap tap <it's they> several of them came with a little man I didn't know *Mr. Robinson* she smiled guiltily <she knows she knows> certainly.

143

Verdict: really bad. <x-ray> said the head doctor pushing a button and illuminating translucent bones. *You can see the stain....the stain right here and* <pointing to me> *a* <a stream of incomprehensible words> *here.*

Take out their tools. Already hooked me up. *It's got to be taken out— we'll have to cut* says the little man. *Mr. Robinson* he says turning toward me <sparse white hair on the narrow bed> *Mr. Robinson* Verdict: a series of frenetic signs follows <I don't understand> • - ••
/ • - •• – – etc.

21.

Monday. Alone. Evening [darkness quotient III]. Ambient shadow > 30°. Curtains closed. *** Syndrome. Fever 99°. Notion of sudden death + hunger.

Tuesday. Mrs. Jones + me. Morning 8:20. 40′ less. Appetite 30%. Evidence of general hearing IV. Curtains open. Light = ± maximum [her blond hair her blond hair].

Wednesday. Outside cold = brain power. Characteristic energy maximum. Excitability of facial muscles. ∅ Syndrome. Hope = 10. Dream of deep summer.

Thursday. Pupil – 1000. Interior plants. Voice breaking + 20. Resilience of spirit (maximum capacity of resistance). Muscle loss. Intra-flesh lesion. Sentimentalism level VIII.

Friday.

```
                        Living
                 /                    \
            light                      rotted
           /     \                    /      \
   [nitrogen]   [grass]           [me]      [grass]
```

Saturday. Mrs. Jones + me. Night quotient. Curtains closed. ° of vegetation = 99. Sonorous elongation. Vocal obfuscation. Average sight. Loss of weight apparent in bony places. Sense of fog.

Sunday. Alone. Vocal access. Persistence of doubles. Temp. 99.5°. Humidity maximum. Developed odor > human threshold normal. Black characteristic: ∞. Sense of disappearance total. % of awareness = 80. Whitening of proximate space maximum.

22. FEBRUARY.

I am a saint. Totally/terminally/on my knees. I tell them: Go... in... (illegible word).

Window on nothing. Black night. And like before. And so on after. Sky black and perfect. Black, and she was right. And the bright yellow field mown hay no light no moon (...). Damp. Empty cool. Black unbeknownst.

I am a saint. *Mr. Robin-son* the small tiny swallowed voice huge shadow of the bed. Not (...) enough. *Mister* minuscule thread disappeared swallowed. Future former fugitive.

I am a completed saint. I am in harmony with nature. Heavy weighted body in the absent grass. Deriving carried current waving grasses under straight light. *Sir oh it's beautiful oh it's beautiful.* Then nothing. Black night.

In the path deep path in the deep forest. There it is. Night cut in two. Lightly disappeared. Divided in all things. *Sir oh it's beautiful oh it's beautiful already small* swallowed voice huge shadow of the bed.

I was going to say I understand. Massive movement of stars. Conjunction of everything. I was going to say I understand. Words for nothing. Like this.

I understand what you said. I understand it all.

Soft warmth and you're no longer moving you're in bed the warm weight of the sheets. The first time that you thought of that. The sound climbing up from outside WHAT'S GOING TO BECOME OF YOU the island of-great-birds the island of sleep.

The place where you touched green grass for the first time. The first time you spoke. I was going to say I understand I'm far away. I understand I'm there here hidden under the leaves. I'm here.

And you're no longer moving. The enchanted island of sleep. The concrete notion. Remember the enormous heat of the spot where for the first time you WHAT'S GOING TO BECOME OF YOU remember the movement of the horse.

I already told you I understand I understand everything. I already told you a line made by walking. Black spiral. Tree mist. Plant-birds. Soft heat and there it is already you're no longer moving. The inter-wall thickness. The exact amount of night WHAT'S GOING TO BECOME OF YOU solid-winter fixed-star grey-zenith.

Decomposed. Son-of-a-bird in yellow field. Much ado about nothing. Heavy weighted body in absent grass. A line made by walking. I was going to say enormous heat of the spot where for the first time.

I already said it yes nothing not a sound. Silence. Nothing. And afterward silence silence. Talala talala. Integral night. Night like before. Like this.

Zero-sum

1.

[alone]

The weather turned magnificent with a
calm whose huge ocean swell rocked soft–
fifteen men including the captain and the
                    but I was born to be
my own destruction

Go! Leave. To leave-morning <Yes! I want to leave> *Oh oh* (tears) *no you can't leave*
<Yes yes> Already morning on deck the cries and seagulls and sperm whales huge
washed air zebra sky. Sky already sky.

– Useless she tells me
he understands your interest perfectly
well by giving his consent to an adven-
more such ideas
and after the welcome tender expressions no
you want to risk your neck
but don't count on our consent
as for me, I'm not about to contribute to your ruin
will never be said that your mother consented
that which your father opposed no

Crossing the garden...tchk-tchk-tchk. Don't turn around sing don't turn around sing
sing the remains of what remains of <oh I'd love to oh I'd love to> *Robin-son Mr.*
Robinson? You can't go back to the house. Sing while crossing <I'm alone that's
me> night behind night of animals. Sing.

[sung]

Oh I'd love to
Oh I'd love to

I am the only
that's me–

I-I
who

no one
no one

acacias
Bzzz

Green planks
and it disappears

beneath the paint here
small woods
naked

The long song between the trees <ouf ouf ouf> the dark growing along under the ivy
the shadow <ouf ouf ouf> *Mister Robinson?* Small voice suspended between the
trees far the flight of steps lit small stain at the back small voice last words low
already far away running behind the dark <ouf ouf ouf> slalom between the branch-
es calculate the trajectories <ouf ouf ouf> *Mis—ter Ro—bin—son?* voice too small
inaudible minuscule already nothing dust to sing

[sung]

the sharpest
really
Among the flowers
that–

Silence
– come out of there

I-I oh but (...)
                            oh

Ended
the roses
                  time now

& roses) and the roses

See you soon everyone
conclusion
dear–

unimaginable if
? his destination

if

Good bye that's all
good bye.

2.

[spoken]

The bee...active...industrious
the flower...beautiful...perfumed
the windows, the sideboards...the tables
nature comes alive... each one
risen warm... light... the river
rising, rolling in its rapid waters

[sung]

The road... long
earth alongside the ditch
pines

[spoken]

... applied
drowned horizon of
... gather at the foot of the trees, the
who... of beautiful voices... gather
the songs... of white feather

He... he asks... what he's going to say
who... to what... you think
... that he's been given
dissipates to
reduction
and as soon as
the sky to darken
and mixed to the crack-
oh I'm scared oh what to do

Items to know. Take everything back <My name is X.> interesting you must admit!

beginning of speech etc. Lessons in leaving. *Mister R.?* Yessss. Bird-movement. Wing crisis that's it. We're there. Keep it up *Mister R.?* Yes-sss I'm listening.

To leap up to run gives him energy
good answer
muscles

and my tears stop halfway in falling
I sense
who reminds me of my
– tell me the name of

For those who
a story that
that protects them

the first objects
of a deep sleep

"Mister
...gallop?"

To leap up
to leap up
The organism

Suddenly to...the
its fall

...To...to
of memory but he's doing all he can
to know
before a certain date

The water is deep, we
...solid

Yes that's it that's enough just like that eh <the sound of waves> I don't understand oh oh R.? What's good for me? What should I do? <and it's my fault and it's my fault> moaning oh forgive me *Mis-ter Robin-son it's not your fault* <calm down calm down> small soft words small in the background minuscule weak light small stain already in the background behind in the dark butterfly-slalom weakly night night already go back there night behind night *oh-oh Ro-bin-son* nothing already night over over nothing night. Night.

[sung]

You who
– who to be
a small sorrow
... to announce the rain

[spoken]

Dark–
the plane trees
Surface

the drowned
in the silt–
sister

Foliage–
plank

Think
– you fear
that I
– be that he's leaving

Wrapped,
stones–

Oh
– oh

The...
...–

Grey
– the leaves

Light wind
or
– n...mphs.

3.

That year the summer was
meager, furtive, light, blue, pure

Summed up
the grass of the fields

the grass
that the knights
on top of their armor

The Sun being indicated by •
Mercury is represented by å Venus by Ω
Saturn by Δ Uranus by ø Neptune by @

Everything summed up
the grass of the fields was green

by all that so
and leaving

May the heavens favor you
I run you run he runs
I ran we ran I have run
that I run that you run that he run

Sail
– red
very soft a water line

Useless
tears, cries
sighs. Is said of a pain
that makes you cry groan etc.
the list of misfortunes
it's said *from my child they tear out my heart*
from who binds captive enslaved
someone to his pleasures to his passions to his sadn-

Eyes
put a blindfold over the eyes
draw something back with effort a cord a bow

a crossbow a spring the wind

by virtue of a single speed
by virtue of a single speed

this horse-plant
of the *wooded*
space
– this woods?

sky blue
– kind
of cobalt and reduced
From a light blue like that
after rain
air

The forest, or a half-light penetrated
– Forest
planks rafters joists beams

Holding itself in the air and tied to something
to a branch to a rope
= suspended

you
– in sum
flight
fold

substance of a green
fusible-black

To grasp to reach
branch– I could never re–

fish
  stream?

4.

Picture in which one moves closer
to the events

Final
spring preferably we chose spring
the grass is green
sky blue
– kind
of cobalt and reduced
From a light blue

Which deafens
a sound dea–
deafening

The Sun being indicated by ●
Of a mechanism
below the skin the air he exhales
the luminous animal but lighter for the flight

beings
Linnaean sexuality
each collection of organs or tissue
destined to analogous functions

the grass that the knights
– on top of their armor
the forest penetrated by half-light

While it lasts quite a while
heart stopping
no longer getting to the brain
the act of its annihilation

the loss of movement the respira-

The one in which
the sound that constitutes the sigh is produced

Each tree–

occupies the center

me-central
the beautiful green

iris
articulation

Crev-
day
the plains
– the night

decomposes them in part
in the void the same shades that in the air

The path of movement of a projectile
that acts as a support
that finds itself in the middle of another
: statue

holds itself
in the air and tied to something
to a branch to a rope
suspended

equilibrium– a huge
black
liquid at the level of its container. The water

That deafens
a sound dea-
the air the air

Cole Swensen's seven books of poetry include *Such Rich Hour* and *Try*. She has been awarded a National Poetry Series selection, the Iowa Poetry Prize, the S.F. State Poetry Center Book Award, and a Pushcart Prize. Her translations include Cadiot's earlier book *Art Poetic'*, Pascalle Monnier's *Bayart*, and Jean Frémon's *Island of the Dead*.

Roof Books
are published by
Segue Foundation
300 Bowery, New York, NY 10012
For a complete list of back issues,
please visit our website at
segue.org

Roof Books are distributed by
SMALL PRESS DISTRIBUTION
1341 Seventh Avenue, Berkeley, CA. 94710-1403.
Phone orders: 800-869-7553
spdbooks.org

ROOF BOOKS

- Andrews, Bruce. **EX WHY ZEE**. 112p. $10.95.
- Andrews, Bruce. **Getting Ready To Have Been Frightened**. 116p. $7.50.
- Benson, Steve. **Blue Book**. Copub. with The Figures. 250p. $12.50
- Bernstein, Charles. **Islets/Irritations**. 112p. $9.95.
- Bernstein, Charles (editor). **The Politics of Poetic Form**. 246p. $12.95; cloth $21.95.
- Brossard, Nicole. **Picture Theory**. 188p. $11.95.
- Champion, Miles. **Three Bell Zero**. 72p. $10.95.
- Child, Abigail. **Scatter Matrix**. 79p. $9.95.
- Davies, Alan. **Active 24 Hours**. 100p. $5.
- Davies, Alan. **Signage**. 184p. $11.
- Davies, Alan. **Rave**. 64p. $7.95.
- Day, Jean. **A Young Recruit**. 58p. $6.
- Di Palma, Ray. **Motion of the Cypher**. 112p. $10.95.
- Di Palma, Ray. **Raik**. 100p. $9.95.
- Doris, Stacy. **Kildare**. 104p. $9.95.
- Dreyer, Lynne. **The White Museum**. 80p. $6.
- Edwards, Ken. **Good Science**. 80p. $9.95.
- Eigner, Larry. **Areas Lights Heights**. 182p. $12, $22 (cloth).
- Gizzi, Michael. **Continental Harmonies**. 92p. $8.95.
- Goldman, Judith. **Vocoder**. 96p. $11.95.
- Gottlieb, Michael. **Ninety-Six Tears**. 88p. $5.
- Gottlieb, Michael. **Gorgeous Plunge**. 96p. $11.95.
- Greenwald, Ted. **Jumping the Line**. 120p. $12.95.
- Grenier, Robert. **A Day at the Beach**. 80p. $6.
- Grosman, Ernesto. **The XULReader: An Anthology of Argentine Poetry (1981–1996)**. 167p. $14.95.
- Hills, Henry. **Making Money**. 72p. $7.50. VHS videotape $24.95. Book & tape $29.95.
- Huang Yunte. **SHI: A Radical Reading of Chinese Poetry**. 76p. $9.95
- Hunt, Erica. **Local History**. 80 p. $9.95.
- Kuszai, Joel (editor) **poetics@**, 192 p. $13.95.
- Inman, P. **Criss Cross**. 64 p. $7.95.
- Inman, P. **Red Shift**. 64p. $6.
- Lazer, Hank. **Doublespace**. 192 p. $12.
- Levy, Andrew. **Paper Head Last Lyrics**. 112 p. $11.95.
- Mac Low, Jackson. **Representative Works: 1938–1985**. 360p. $12.95, $18.95 (cloth).
- Mac Low, Jackson. **Twenties**. 112p. $8.95.
- Moriarty, Laura. **Rondeaux**. 107p. $8.
- Neilson, Melanie. **Civil Noir**. 96p. $8.95.
- Pearson, Ted. **Planetary Gear**. 72p. $8.95.
- Perelman, Bob. **Virtual Reality**. 80p. $9.95.

ROOF BOOKS
are published by
Segue Foundation, 303 East 8th Street, New York, NY 10009
Visit our website at **segue.org**

ROOF BOOKS are distributed by
SMALL PRESS DISTRIBUTION
1341 Seventh Avenue, Berkeley, CA. 94710-1403.
Phone orders: 800-869-7553
spdbooks.org